Discipline by Design

A Handbook of Proven Steps to Operating Control

Published by Renaissance Business Press Inc.
© 1996 by Paul W. Larson

This publication is designed to provide accurate and authoritative information in regard to the subject matter covered. It is sold with the understanding that the publisher is not engaged in rendering legal, accounting, or other professional advice. If legal advice or other expert assistance is required, the services of a competent professional person should be sought.
- from a declaration of principles jointly adopted by a committee of the American Bar Association and a committee of publishers

Please direct any comments, questions, or suggestions regarding this book to:

Editorial Department
Renaissance Business Press Inc.
16608 San Pedro, Suite 106
San Antonio, TX   78232

Library of Congress Catalog Card Number: 95-92768
Publisher's Cataloging-in-Publication Data
Larson, Paul W
     discipline by design: a handbook of proven steps to operating control
     p.   cm.
     Includes bibliograpgical references and index.
     ISBN 1-888355-06-9
     1. Production management. 2. Just-in time systems. 3. Process control - statistical methods. 4. Manufacturing processes. 5. Communication in management. 6. Visual communications. I. Title
     HD30.29.L19   1996
     658.4'5–dc20
Printed in the United States of America
Printing Number
10 9 8 7 6 5 4 3 2 1

To Charlene

Contents

Continuous Flow Processing

Chart Interpretation and Advanced Techniques

The Visual Factory

Preface

This book was put together to outline from practical experience some remedies to the problems of growth and controlling that growth. It is light on theory and centered on actual case histories that have occurred over the years in my own experience in managing the operating activities of "job shop" businesses in four distinctly different industries.

The material is not designed to be broadly applied to any number of applications. It is pointed to the small and growing company, plant, or division that has reached a sales level of about ten to twenty million dollars annually and is beginning to experience a loss of control brought on by growth.

There are four key aspects to managing a business that are covered. They are planning, execution of the plan, controlling, and providing feedback. For an organization to get back into some semblance of control, each of these four areas has to be explored, understood, mastered, and then integrated with the other three.

Each of these disciplines is viewed in general terms with some real case histories included as enlightening examples. There is not enough here to master any of these, and that is by design.

I wanted the main focus of this work to be one of illustrating the interdependence of these four areas. None can stand alone and lead an organization to success. Each must be understood then woven into an overall scheme of management that matches the remedy to the appropriate situation.

As with many other things in life, there is no correlation here between the length of writing on a topic and that subject's importance.

The section on planning is relatively short and yet that is the most important part of the business in terms of being able to bring dollars to the bottom line. Much of the material on planning is the result of an enlightening experience I had in 1985 when I was able to visit a Toyota managed automobile assembly plant. In the matter of a few short hours, fifteen years of education and experience up to that point merged with what I was seeing to form a clear picture of what a good planning and execution system for a job shop would look like. I know that clarity would not be there now were it not for that visit.

The chapters on statistical process control are quite a bit longer because there are a number of different aspects to understand. The return here is smaller though because you are fixing problems that may have been prevented altogether with better planning.

That being understood, all of these sections are equally important. Wherever possible I have indicated the sources of particular subjects covered. In most cases, these sources were the charts and tables commonly used in the plants I was working in. A comprehensive bibliography in the back offers more to those who want to read more on any of these topics.

This book is written and laid out so it can be used as a source of lesson plans and illustrations for plant or company training programs. It's main purpose is to provide some clarity into an approach to achieving good operational control to managers whose background and levels of experience leave them relatively untested in the area of operations management.

Paul W. Larson
San Antonio, Texas

Planning the Business

Bullfight critics row on row
Crowd the vast arena full
But only one man's there who knows
And he's the man who fights the bull

Author unknown

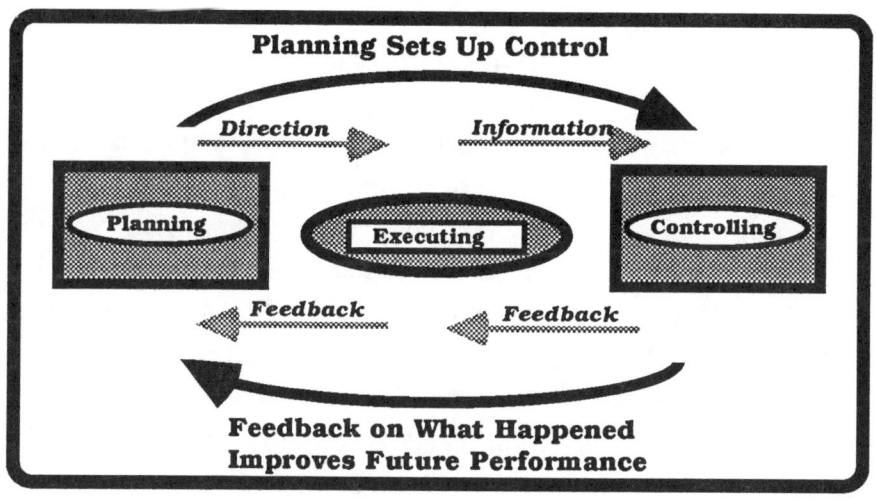

Growth and Planning

This little diagram that looks like it came out of a business school textbook looks very simple and obvious but it has a lot of power to it. In running a growing business, these items are self apparent and they don't have to be explained in any great detail. The problem arises when the business starts to grow.

What used to be able to be kept in the head of the person running the organization is now too large for that kind of mental control. Not only is it too large, unless the thought processes are very organized, there is no integrated scheme of things and control is lost.

Instead of one person, there are departments or at least different people assuming these responsibilities. Where once, one knew all, there are now several who see only their part. Not only do they have to learn how to use and share information together, they have to be able to relate as well. This all has to be mastered and understood by those charged with the overall responsibility for an operation for they are the ones facing the Bull.

For a company to succeed as it grows, it has to develop systems to do what people used to do when it was smaller. The systems that are going to be covered here are not new. What is new is this approach to show how interdependent they are and how they fit into this overall scheme of factory control. This is a scheme in which the connections that were lost in growing the business out of the understanding in one person's mind are reconnected and reintegrated again.

10

Planning and Control Systems

Quite often a growing company will look outside to a high powered executive (at considerable expense) to get the management capacity to bring the the business under control again. The wherewithal to attract such a capable person can place quite a strain on the finances of a small company. Such a move can also be a shock to key people already in the organization who are looking for operating systems to solve their problems and get a new boss instead.

An alternative is to implement the systems described here with the help of an experienced facilitator. This can be done at a fraction of the cost and the resulting policies and practices can serve as a bridge until larger sales revenues are realized. At that time it can be determined if this type of hire is necessary. This can often be implemented immediately without the addition of what many call a "plateau hire" or the addition of someone of medium stature who eventually will have to be replaced with more growth.

These are simple and easy to use principles that can be used by the existing staff to improve planning, executing, and controlling activities. At some point in time the caliber of management issue will have to be addressed but with this approach, that will be later and not sooner.

Here is that same diagram again only this time it shows the actual management systems we will be using to accomplish each of these activities.

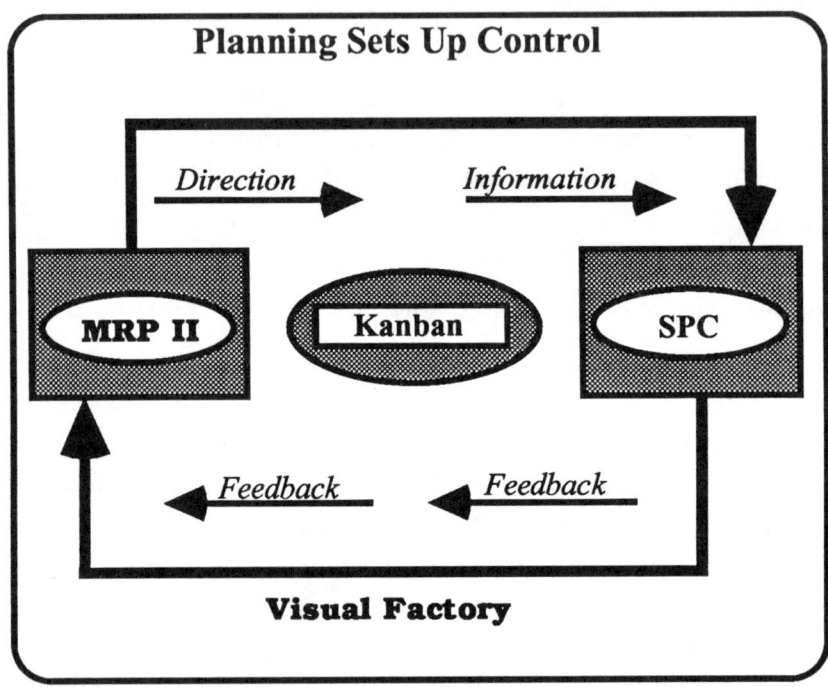

Definitions

As a means of some introductory definitions, **MRP II** is the abbreviation for Manufacturing Resource Planning. It is an integrated approach to business planning that integrates and involves all parts of the business. It is commonly confused with a computer system because computers are frequently used extensively. It is actually a business planning system involving people. It is the way the connections that were lost with the establishment of separate planning, controlling and administrative activities are reconnected again.

In a small company it can be administered without a computer but as the business grows, computers will eventually have to be used to keep up with all the necessary information transactions.

Kanban, flow processing or **pull systems** all describe the same basic principle that is used to execute the plan. They are based on lean supply chains and described in detail later.

Statistical Process Control or **S P C** for short is the methodology used to pick up the pieces as to what went wrong with the plan and how can it be improved. It gives us information in a statistical sense so we not only know what is going on, we get some good guidance as to just how significant each of the bits of information we are looking at are. It is used extensively in Quality Control.

Where Good Planning Originates

The whole process, however, begins with a **vision.** It is absolutely imperative that the present top manager, owner, family, or group have a clear vision of what the company will be. This could be a vision of how it should look, perform, grow, just be, or any key aspect that is important to whoever is at the top.

Planning the Business

Everything that will come in the future will be driven from this vision. Clarity is important and it will be necessary to have some consistency about it over time so the aspects of the company that are flowing from it are stable also.

Quite often it takes several years for everything to come together and crystallize in the form of a vision but once it does there will be a clarity and focus that was not there before.

Leaders will have to prepare themselves for this responsibility. Beginning with their own expectations in light of what they see in their organization and the competitive world it faces, they must prepare themselves and then begin to educate others in the organization.

Then, as with any good training program, they must see that the organization begins to lose "wait". The organization must find and root out the delays that are keeping it from reducing lead times to the marketplace.

When that's done, provide a vision to help the organization lose "weight". Eliminate the non value added activities from the organization and remove them permanently.

If a clear vision does not seem to be present, or if it seems to change frequently it probably means that some reading on the subject, discussions with others in the same types of situation, and visits to as many similar and dissimilar operations as possible is necessary in order to get a grasp of the different ways in which the top person was able to formulate a vision.

This is probably the most difficult part of the whole process because after the vision is set, those at the top will be constantly measured as to whether it was appropriate given the circumstances the company was faced with at the time.

Communicating the Vision

Given that the vision is right on target as to what is needed and timing, the next step is to articulate that vision in a very clear and concise vision statement. This vision statement provides the framework that is used to initiate a strategic planning process that defines the purpose of the organization, provides direction for future products and services, and develops a competitive strategy.

Only time will tell if the vision was effective. The point here is that it should be able to be expressed simply and drive the company.

Sales and Operations Planning

A process that can begin right away even before the vision statement is sales and operations planning. Over time, it should show a sales plan and corresponding operations plan that fit well with the vision statement. In the meantime it doesn't hurt to get started before the vision statement is ready because even without the vision you're going to have to deal with the future and this is the way to do it.

If, at a later date, you come up with a vision statement that is not congruent with the sales and operations plan, you can begin whatever planning steps necessary to bring the two into line.

Planning sets up control. Those with the most accurate picture of the future will be in the best position to capitalize on the opportunities as they see them. Companies are under good control today because the events they are experiencing were predicted far enough in the past so they have been able to put all the required resources in place to deal with them in a timely manner. When you begin to lose accuracy in your picture of the future you begin to lose the timing necessary to bring things into place to deal with today's events. Eventually you get to the point where it is too late to bring something in (i.e. inventory) to deal with the situation and the situation overwhelms you.

Forecasting

The best insurance for a good picture of the future is an accurate **sales forecast.** It is the company's crystal ball that's going to predict the future. The more accurate the prediction, the more profitable the future. The forecast should be the responsibility of the top individual in the company who is closest to the customer. Normally it is the sales manager.

An accurate forecast is so valuable that there are many who recommend that up to forty percent of the forecaster's bonus potential be directly tied to forecast accuracy. This helps encourage a deeper knowledge of the intentions of the customer base. It also guards against setting a low forecast and then looking good by beating it or setting an unrealistically high forecast with very little chance of hitting it.

There are whole volumes on how to attain an accurate forecast through methods as sophisticated as complex statistical sampling to more simpler methods such as polling the customer base. A wide variety of these methods should be explored and understood because this is where the gold is.

In setting up the forecast format, there should be a few months of history shown before the current month and several (at least twelve) months of future predictions by product lines. Each month the earliest month of history is dropped off and a new month out into the future is added to the forecast. The present month and one month out are frozen so forecast accuracy can be measured when those sales actually come in. The forecast for all other months can be changed as needed. In some cases, the forecast would be for quarters but since most use months, months are referred to here.

With the forecast complete, the **sales and operations planning process** can begin. This starts with a meeting that should be chaired by the top manager and it is run monthly as soon as possible after the close of the previous month. If it is held much later than that it is easy to digress into a meeting of how we are doing in the present month rather than a review and measurement of the forecast and planning for the future.

If the forecast is less than the business plan then **sales planning** kicks into play with planned actions on the part of the sales function to bring the forecast back up to the business plan. If it is determined to be unlikely, then the business plan is revised to the forecast. With this revision come changes to the fundamental base of the business, usually with reductions in personnel, inventories, marginal assets, and capital spending.

Using the sales and operations planning format though, these revisions to the business plan will come early rather than late.

Planning the Business

Here is a suggested format for a sales forecast.

Period Number	1	2	3	4	5	6	7	8	9	10	11	12
Sales Forecast												
Actual Sales												
Deviation												
Planned Prod												
Actual Prod												
Deviation												
Inventory Plan												
Actual												
Deviation												

The **operations planning** part of this function also begins with the updated forecast. If the forecast is in line with the business plan then things are on schedule and no changes are made. If the forecast was light, then inventory, people, and capital plans are reduced accordingly.

If the forecast shows a much higher than anticipated level of sales then there is a one week period for review. If, after that

18

review, it is determined there are insufficient resources planned to meet the revised forecast, a decision is made to either invest in bringing these resources in, or revise the forecast back down to the original business plan with a note as to why this revision was made.

If there are no changes from operations proposed one week after the forecast then the company goes with the revised forecast under the assumption that is achievable and will occur.

The only stipulation in this process is the planning horizon must be sufficient to plan all resources effectively.

Forecast accuracy of ninety percent or better is considered acceptable.

Data Integrity

The company has to run off a **single data base.** Different departments cannot be using different sales estimates etc., or the company will never achieve full integration. Using the single data base is the first step to reconnecting the different entities that were fragmented with the growth of the company.

Some obstacles to using a single data base are;

- One department doesn't believe the forecast so it uses its own set of expectations as a basis for ordering materials etc.
- The information system has not kept pace with the company's growth.
- The software selected does not fit the company.

- Inventory, Bill of material, and routing drivers are not accurate.

A single data base is necessary and should be used by all functions for financial planning, reporting, and measurement and should come right off the operating system.

Using the Information

The forecast that results from the sales and operations planning process should be loaded into the operating system. Simulations and projections can be made to show planned purchases, inventories, people requirements, and potential capital requirements.

Basically, the operating system is going to ask, and you will have the answer to the following questions.

> What are we going to make? (sell or do)
> What does it take to make it?
> What do we have?
> What do we have to get?

The quality of the future control of the company rests in the quality of the answers for each of these questions. As has often been said, predicting the future is easy. Trying to figure out what's going on now...........now that's hard!

The first question, What are we going to make?" is answered monthly by the **sales forecast**. Since the effectiveness of the control we expect to have over the company in the future is the direct result of the foresight of the plan the company is operating under, the answer to this question, that is to say the quality of the answer is extremely important.

In the very long view, this first question is also answered by the **strategic vision** set for the company. The company will focus on doing things right but time will tell if the company was doing the right things.

In any case, the more accurate the answer that can be given to this first question, the more success we can expect from the company because, as will be seen, the greatest part of the planning process depends on this first question.

Once we know what it is we are going to make, we need to know what it takes to make it. This would be the materials, labor, capital, and any other resources required to make the product. The operating system should have this information loaded so it can begin its search once it receives the forecast.

Bills of material are needed that accurately list what materials the product will require. Existing bills of material will have to be reviewed for accuracy and new bills should be carefully scrutinized.

If **Bills of labor** arc used, the same holds true for them also.

Routings which show the work centers the products move through must also be reviewed for accuracy. Since each of these areas is more controllable than the forecast, we will be looking for ninety-eight percent accuracy here.

So when it comes to answering the question: "What does it take to make it?"; the operating system just has to search the accurate Bills of material and routings to provide a very accurate answer.

What do we have? If the inventory records are highly accurate the operating system can swing through them and answer this question accurately as well. If the records are not highly accurate the quality of the answer to this question will be at the level of the records accuracy.

Cycle Counting

We have to use cycle counting as a mechanism to gain and maintain inventory record accuracy. There are four aspects to cycle counting that are important to the running of the business.

The first is that it discovers the causes of errors. When an inventory error is discovered, you not only fix the record, you go back to the transaction that caused the error and correct what caused that improper transaction. The cause could be insufficient training, a security problem, a problem with the software, or whatever. Whatever it is, find the cause of the error and correct it so it doesn't happen again.

Another is that it measures results. Done daily, with the results visibly posted, it very visibly lets everyone know if the inventory records are sufficiently accurate. We are looking for at least ninety-five percent accuracy here. This is one area that can be audited frequently by the accounting department to verify that the records are as accurate as we say they are.

A third thing cycle counting can do is correct inaccurate records. Whenever a cycle count does not match the record on the operating system, the items should be recounted. If it is still off, the record in the computer must be adjusted.

Lastly, you can eliminate the annual inventory. The sole purpose of this activity is to verify the balance sheet, not make the records accurate. In doing so, many inventories make the records less accurate, not more, through errors made in the taking of the inventory. Although the elimination of the expense of the inventory is desirable, it is the elimination of these counting errors that gives us a better system.

All this becomes practical once the ninety-five percent accuracy level has been reached on a location by location basis.

Once the operating system is loaded with the up to date forecast, reviews the bills of material and routing files to see what the requirements are, and checks the inventory file to see what we have, it is ready to answer the last question. **What do we have to get?**

This then becomes our plan for bringing in people, inventory, and any equipment needed. This is where we stop talking about what we are going to do and start spending actual dollars. It's fairly clear to see now that the wisdom of these expenditures is directly related to the accuracy of the forecast, Bills of Material, and inventories. If this information is not accurate, all we are doing is taking bad information and moving it through our operating system at the speed of light.

Using the Operating System

With a high level of accuracy in all this activity, however, the operating system can be used to project income statements and balance sheets over the life of the forecast.

So, as a quick review, there should be a vision and vision statement that is used to initiate a strategic planning process that defines the company's purpose, provides direction to new products and services, and develops a competitive strategy.

There is a monthly sales and operations planning process that is derived from this that is run by the top manager and covers a planning horizon sufficient to cover the planning for all resources effectively. A single data base is used by all functions for reporting, measurement, and financial planning and this comes right off the operating system.

Simulations and projections are then made from the results of the sales and operations planning process that go beyond requirements planning into planned profit statements and balance sheets.

When you look at these planned financial statements your next concern will be how close they will be. Once you dwell on that question for a while you will have a very deep understanding as to why the accuracies referred to are so important and why they should be measured and tracked.

We now have a well developed and accurate operating plan so we can expect to be under good control in the future.

Common Reasons for Failure

. . . . But not quite. The most important part of this plan is the relationship it has with the control process. A good plan will develop reference points that set up the control process in the company.

Plans that fail to do this usually do so for one or more of the following reasons.

• The planning is not integrated into the operating system.

• The different dimensions of planning have not been understood.

• Management at all levels is not engaged in the planning activities.

• Responsibility for planning is vested solely in one individual or a planning department.

• Management expects the plans to come true as planned.

• Too much is attempted at once.

• Management fails to operate by the plan.

• Extrapolation and financial projections are confused with planning.

• Inadequate information inputs are used.

• Too much emphasis is placed on only one aspect of planning.

These reasons are self explanatory and they provide a good checklist to use in evaluating the communication of your strategic vision and your sales and operations planning activities.

The Planning Cycle

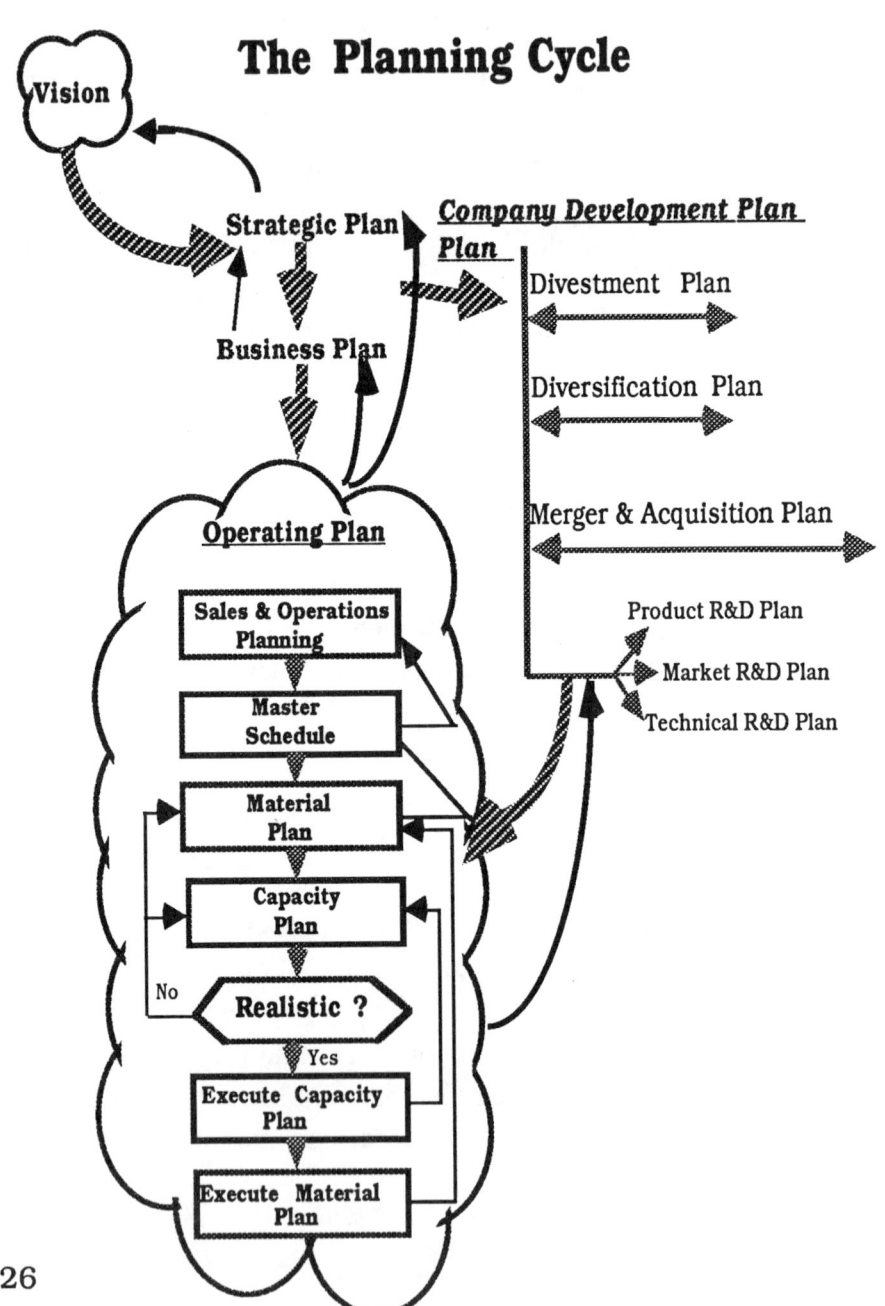

Control Versus Controls

We have now completed the first phase in establishing control over the operation but we are not under control yet. From the plan we have established reference marks where we intend to be in the future. We have plotted a course and can now measure where we are going compared to plan.

This plan is one of the controls we will be using but it doesn't mean we are under control yet. The similarity of the ring of the words control and controls is misleading and must be viewed in the following way.

The word controls is not the plural of the word control. The two words have different meanings altogether. More controls do not necessarily give more control. The synonyms for controls are measurement and information and the synonym for control is direction.

It is this sense of direction that intertwines control with the management function of planning. In this scheme, the planning process sets up the nature of the control.

Control can also be described as the state of the company, a result.

Controls on the other hand, are boundaries for the facts and events that describe an organization. They provide a source for the feedback that is so important in the control process.

Where many companies get sidetracked is in trying to get control by the use of more controls. If action plans can solve a problem, then five of them are better and twenty pounds of them will give you an excellent company.

Not so.

If you can focus in on where you are in relationship to your plan and how you got there you will achieve a much higher state of control than if you just focus in on a lot of controls.

Feedback to the Plan

Feedback is the term used to describe the information coming out of the control process. In the later sections on statistical process control you will see many different ways in which this information can be gathered and displayed.

Control cannot be achieved without feedback. This is because control functions operate through the feedback of information from important points of performance to you, the decision maker.

Here is that flow diagram shown earlier showing the relationships among planning, executing the plan, and controlling.

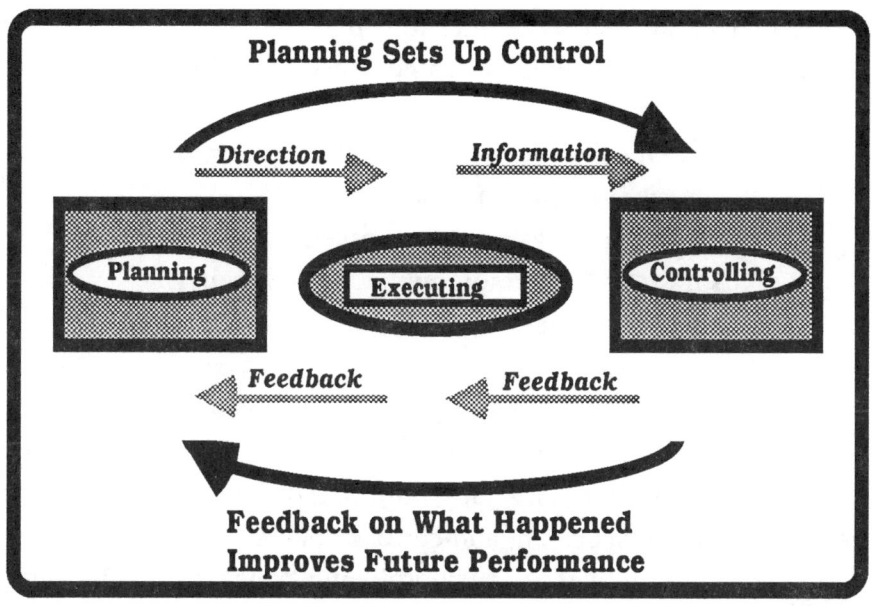

The feedback on what has happened is integrated back into the planning process so that future plans are improved as a result of that learning.

There are four basic questions that have to be satisfactorily answered before the feedback can be considered adequate.

1. Is the feedback telling us where the progress towards objectives is being hindered?
2. Is it going to everyone concerned?
3. Is it timely? (the more immediate the better)
4. Is it continuous?

Everyone needs to know where the problems are as soon as possible after they are discovered. They also need to have this information continuously and not as a knee jerk reaction to management's most current number one concern.

If they can't get to every problem at once, that's OK. They still need the visibility that the other problems remain out there.

Visual Controls

The most effective way to communicate this feedback is by using simple, clear, and easy to understand visual means posted up throughout the company. These highlights viewed here are covered in great detail in the last section on the visual factory.

The principle behind this fact is that the most effective control is self control. If the information is complete and timely, responsible people will control themselves.

They will not need frequent briefings as to whether they are doing well or poorly. They will know how well they are doing and chances are they are already doing something about those situations where the feedback is showing problems.

Here are some examples of feedback for visual control.

- Safety .....General information, Right to Know, Material Safety Data Sheets, Department and individual safety performance.
- Organization Chart .....Updated *daily* if necessary to show each person in the company or department.
- Attendance performance by individual.
- Training status by individual.
- The plan for the year. Post results against the plan.
- General Personnel information.
- Vacation schedules.
- Quality and delivery performance levels.
- Maintenance: Scheduled and performed.
- Planned equipment additions and when.
- Individual and department production performance Include training curves and instructions for the new people.
- Customer feedback.
- Current promotions for products for that department.

The Least Worst Decision

Part of the planning process requires that some decisions must be made quickly from several alternatives that are either risky or otherwise less than attractive. A paralysis from analysis can occur if decision makers are unable to move off of this dilemma and recognize the need to make a difficult decision. This is what is known as a least worst decision.

As a manager you are rarely called upon to make the easy decisions. The choices to those are so readily apparent that they are usually made much farther down in the organization. If you find yourself making a lot of these easy decisions you may want to take another look at just how much control you have really delegated to your staff. The choices you will be called upon to make are quite often between two or more ugly alternatives.

There are two problems with these types of decisions that are best managed with good planning and feedback communications. The first is how to get the decision maker on to the business of making the business decision and away from agonizing over the lack of better alternatives or from wasting even more time looking for a nonexistent but more pleasant alternative.

The second is to get the organization itself to recognize the lack of easy, pleasant alternatives.

A format that is helpful early in the planning process is as follows.

1. Define all the possible events that may occur.
2. Determine the actions that can be taken.
3. Determine the value (in dollars or utility) of each possible combination of events.
4. Assign a probability to each of those events that reflects your degree of uncertainty.

5. Find the expected value of each alternative action by multiplying its value by the assigned probability.

6. Select the alternative with the highest expected value.

Planning and Uncertainty

Those who are shaken by having to look out into the future to make decisions can get some comfort from a structural approach like this. As in this example.

We have to decide whether to build another large new plant in Pittsburgh or expand the existing one. Subsequent market conditions will determine the profit that can be made. It is possible to build a small plant and expand it later when more about the market demand is known. The cost of the expansion would be Three million dollars but it would be able to supply a high market demand and obtain the same ten million dollar profits that we could get by building the larger plant now.

Right now, we want to know whether to build large or small and later decide to expand the small plant.

First, we put this information into a decision tree.

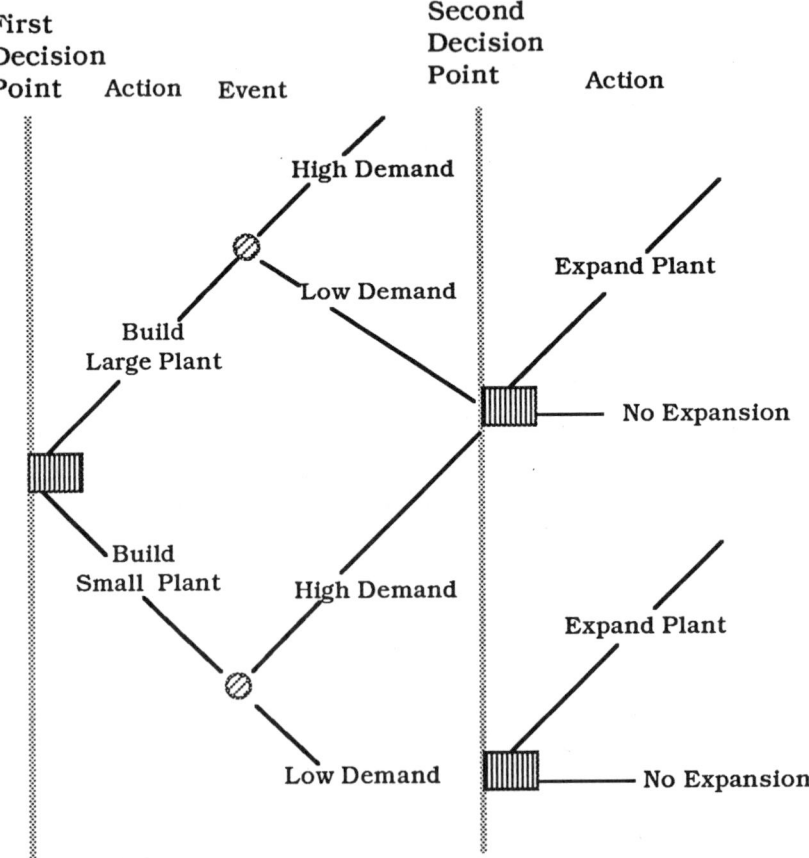

We think there is a sixty percent chance for high demand (.6) and a forty percent chance for low demand (.4). The large plant with high demand will have a six million dollar profit and if the demand is low it will be one million dollars.

The lower cost of the small plant limits the high demand revenue to four million dollars but raises the low demand revenue to three million dollars from much lower operating costs.

If the smaller plant is expanded later it can earn a slightly lower five million dollars at high demand due to the less efficient costs of constructing what would eventually be a large plant.

Now we have a decision tree that looks like this.

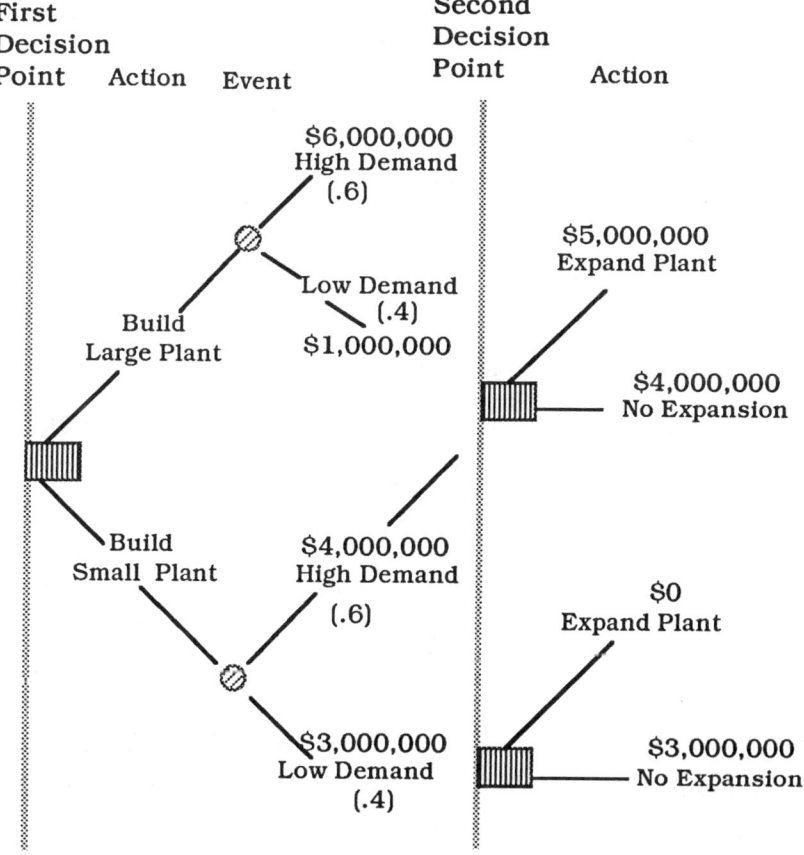

First Decision Point   Action   Event   Second Decision Point   Action

$6,000,000 High Demand (.6)

$5,000,000 Expand Plant

Low Demand (.4) $1,000,000

Build Large Plant

$4,000,000 No Expansion

Build Small Plant

$4,000,000 High Demand (.6)

$0 Expand Plant

$3,000,000 Low Demand (.4)

$3,000,000 No Expansion

Planning the Business

The reduced decision tree becomes;

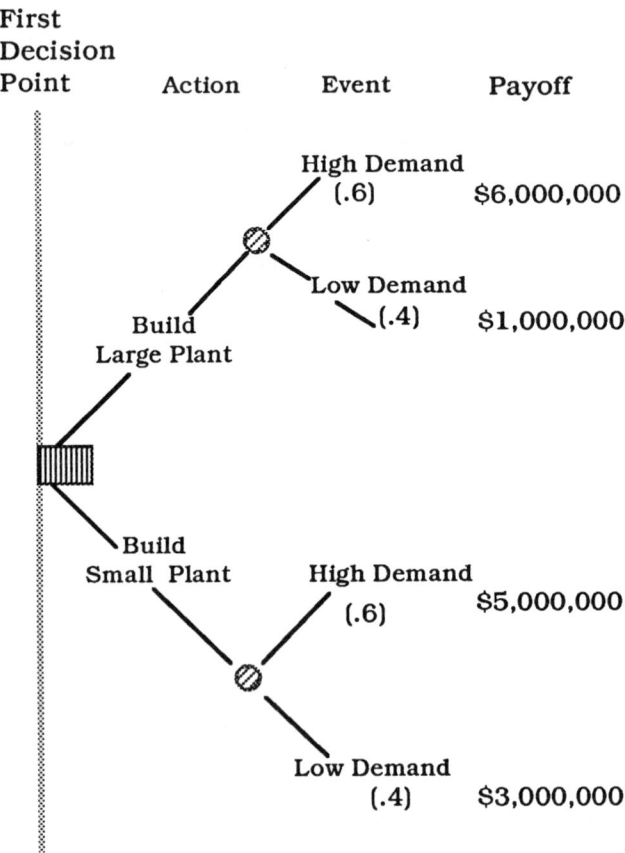

We are now deciding whether or not to build a large or small plant because we know we can always expand the small plant at a later date.

Here's the final decision tree.

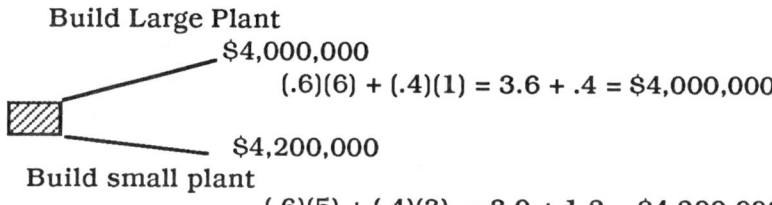

Build Large Plant
$4,000,000
(.6)(6) + (.4)(1) = 3.6 + .4 = $4,000,000

$4,200,000
Build small plant
(.6)(5) + (.4)(3) = 3.0 + 1.2 = $4,200,000

This means the best decision is to build a small plant and expand it later if the high market demand materializes. Without looking at the plant expansion possibility with its assigned probability, the exact opposite conclusion could have been reached earlier.

Building probabilities like this into your own decision trees can help in dealing with the uncertainties of the future.

Planning Versus Forecasting

Planning is not the same thing as forecasting. Forecasting is limited to fairly short time spans and planning goes out beyond there. Long range planning becomes necessary because forecast accuracy suffers the farther out into the future you look.

Planning deals with the question of what has to be done today to be prepared for an uncertain future. This is different from planning for what we will actually do. In the planning sense, the question is not as much what will happen in the future as it is a consideration of what has to be factored into what we are thinking and doing today so the company can be around in the future.

There is risk in the future and attempts to minimize or eliminate that risk can be futile. By definition, you are taking some risks in the expectation of achieving some sort of reward. Generally, the higher the risk, the higher the reward.

The question then becomes asking if the risks being taken are the *right* risks.

The end result of long range planning then is the ability to assume a greater risk, for this risk taking is the only way to improve innovation and entrepreneurial performance. Otherwise, you are just doing what the others are doing with no real differentiation that can allow you to stand out.

To be successful, a company must know and understand the risks that it faces. Its management must be able to make informed choices among risk taking actions rather than just move obediently ahead based on instinct, hearsay, or a guess.

Planning Versus Budgeting

Planning is also not the same thing as budgeting. Budgeting is really the result of a plan. A budget is a formal quantitative expression of the planning that management has completed.

It is the result of a series of planning decisions that came from this rigorous look at the sales and operations plan and beyond.

Budgeting has benefits of its own such as;

1. Because it formalizes responsibilities and future measurement, it compels managers to think ahead.
2. Budgeting provides expectations that can serve as a framework for evaluating future performance.
3. Budgeting can aid in coordinating management efforts so the objectives of the whole company can be in harmony with the objectives of its various departments.

Since budgets normally run for twelve month periods, there are times such as the end of the present year when the new budget hasn't been assembled yet, that the formal look out into the future is only a few short months.

If the budget were the only planning device the company was using, this could create dangerous holes in the company's overall planning.

Continuous Flow
Processing

This time, like all times, is a very good one,
if we but know what to do with it

Ralph Waldo Emerson

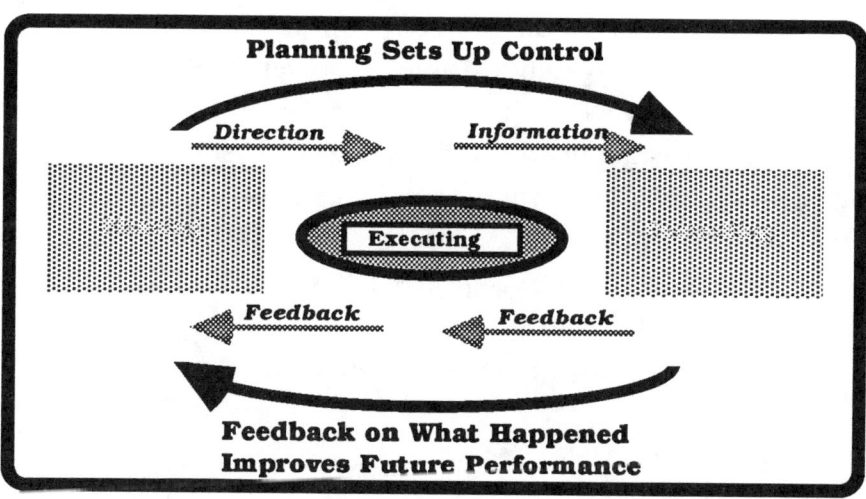

Where Delays Occur

When you have reduced your lead times to the absolute minimum and are running your company or department with the absolute minimum of materials required you have optimized the flow of your process. Continuous flow is a way to describe how that optimization looks when it has been achieved. To get there requires quite a shift in thinking as well as how the flow of the process is set up. As both go against the conventional wisdom there is usually a lot of disbelief and resistance to the changes involved.

First, let's really look at lead times. How long does it take to go from receipt of the order, through the whole process, and out to ship to the customer? In a process we will look at here, the lead times presently being quoted to the customers is thirty working days in an industry where that is a little bit better than the norm.

The question that begs the answer is what happens during those thirty days? The order has to be entered, tooling has to be prepared, injected, and a shell made, it has to be cast and if it is a marine fitting it also has to be plated, it has to be packed, and it has to be shipped. How long does all of this activity take?

For a 144 piece Casting order we have:

Order entry	1/8 day
Tooling	5 days
Wax Injection	1/8day
Shell	5 Days
Foundry	1/2 day
Plating	1 day
Pack	1/8 day
Ship	1/8 day
Total processing time	**12 Days**

It takes about twelve days to do everything that has to be done with this order yet the customer is being told it takes thirty days. What gives?

Principles of Continuous Flow

Uncoupling

Well first of all, something has to stand between the difference in the demand a market can make and the ability of a company to respond to that demand. If not, the results would be chaos because of the simple fact most shops cannot match the volatility of the market on a step by step basis. It is a lot easier to *say* you want to buy one million of something than it is to make that something.

It is the principle of **uncoupling** that stands between the shop's need to have a fairly level load and the market's inherent ups and downs. This uncoupling is usually accomplished with lead times although there are some instances such as commodity products where this is accomplished with price changes.

To make a company totally responsive to all potential changes in market demand would be impractical because the costs of carrying the necessary excess capacity could never be covered by the existing business and unless the existing customer base would be willing to pay a premium for that insurance capacity, that company would eventually fail.

Continuous Flow

There are some steps that can be taken though because clearly the largest single reason for the long lead time is the time the order spends waiting for each next operation.

For instance, where is it written that an engineering department can only work one shift? In manufacturing, multi shift operations are common where the capital requirements are high and can only be recovered through higher utilization. Why not the same concept on other parts of the organization where the opportunity costs of the long lead times are also quite high and can be recovered only by more utilization of the time available?

It makes no sense that an order should sit over night with no work being done on it because that department traditionally does not work a second shift. This is the first lesson of continuous flow. **Let the flow be continuous.** Use as much of the twenty four hour clock as possible to keep the orders moving through all parts of the company all of the time.

A normal second shift is typically hard to maintain with any continuity of qualified people because, after all, the hours are pretty ugly compared to the daytime alternatives. One way around this is to schedule forty hours a week on Monday through Thursday. You are not going to ship on Friday nights anyway because most trucking companies don't ship then and most customer's typically don't receive on weekends.

It has been shown that the prospect of three day weekends all year long except for temporary busy periods is enough to offset the unattractiveness of working those hours.

Another finding has been improved attendance. It seems the difference in losing one quarter (10/40) of a paycheck is enough of a penalty over one fifth (8/40) of a paycheck to promote better attendance records. It also solves the problem of no shows on Friday nights.

Flexibility

Another principle of continuous flow is to **flex as much as possible** with the ebb and flow of the work. Flexible hours and maintaining some overcapacity are two of the ways this is accomplished.

If you find yourself running departments on fairly regular eight hour schedules even though your activity rate is much higher during some part of the week than another, you are not doing a good job of matching your capacity up with the demand. Flex your work schedule as much as possible to reflect this variation in demand. That way there will be no build up of orders unattended to during the times the business flow is out of sync with your staffing practices.

It may mean some ten hour days and some eight and six hour days but that's one of the keys to continuous flow. When the work is there you have to be ready for it and when the flow rate changes, you have to adjust to the extent possible.

Demand Pull Systems

When you talk about traffic, people can easily understand what you are saying when you mention rush hour or holiday traffic and how it can affect them. They relate right away to the pain and suffering of slugging it out on a crowded highway and taking forever to get where they are going. They even have to leave much earlier than normal because their "lead times" will be much longer. They can easily see the difference between those conditions and an empty highway where they can just breeze along and get to where they are going with hardly any "lead time".

Put the same people in a production setting and they will think nothing of jamming the shop floor with much more work than it can handle during any given period. They will maintain that it is "motivational" for people to see a lot of work to do and they will feel secure in knowing there is so much work there. This may or may not be so. Maybe toll collectors are more motivated and feel more secure during a rush hour. In any case your orders are in a rush hour and that is a reason your lead times are longer than they need be.

The solution to this situation is to use a **demand pull** philosophy in setting up the flow of your process. Work cannot move downstream until the downstream operation is clear and reaches back for it. If they are not ready for it,   **STOP!!!** Do not keep producing and pushing work on them. They won't be able to do anything to it and only bad things can happen to it. It can get lost, damaged, run out of sequence, or pulled ahead of a critical order if it is an easy job. With a pull system, that does not happen.

Kanban, just in time, and continuous flow have been used to describe this type of system. Here is an example of a simple Kanban type of system.

Packaging is received in bales or units of 240 each. Each unit has a load tag. There is enough space set aside on the production floor for two units. When a unit is pulled into production, the load tag is removed and sent to purchasing. That is the signal to bring in one more unit. If both units are consumed during the day, two load tags are sent to purchasing to be replaced before the next day begins. If the rate of consumption is too fast for the replenishment rate an additional buffer stock is added so production never runs out of material.

Buffers like this can usually be avoided if the supplier is situated locally. The supplier should have your MRP plan so it knows what to have ready for you within the bounds of your own forecast accuracy. If you are reasonably accurate in your forecasting and regularly give your supplier a few months of visibility into the future, and pick up material to that plan on a regular basis, would there ever be a good reason for that supplier not to have that material when you need it? Imagine the potential inventory turns.

Since you are only bringing in what you have consumed, you can never have too much inventory. An ideal situation would be to have the supplier next door and prepared to have you pick up on demand. A small truck or even a fork truck goes over every two hours to pick up what is needed. Do that four times in an eight hour shift and you have turned your inventory four times. Do this every day for a 240 working day year and you will have turned your packaging inventory 960 times. Compare this with where you are at and that is the potential for improvement right up to the ideal.

Logistics and distance may dictate fewer and larger pickups but the principle is the same. Replenish only what you have used, give your supplier good planning information, and the supply will always be there.

Push Systems

Kanban is very different from what is called a push system. This is sometimes called finite capacity planning or finite scheduling. It is the progress of about twenty years development of materials and software systems that promote the approach that a thoroughly planned computer based shop floor control system is the ultimate. The power of the computer has generated the capability for very detailed schedules for making or buying whatever you need. It is a push system in that it is the schedule that pushes people into making or buying what is needed and it is the schedule that pushes the parts through the system. Material requirements planning or **MRP** is an example of this type of system

Though this type of detailed scheduling system seems like good management, there is some guesswork involved. You need to guess how long it will take for everything in the plan to happen, how many people will be absent, if any machines will break down, if some purchased material is of such poor quality that it cannot be used etc. The shop floor control system allows corrections to be made daily but bad guesses can still result in excess inventory.

Even so, the improvements in inventory and production control with MRP were so great that it set the standard for shop floor control for many years, hence its popularity.

Until the last few years, it seemed that this early success of MRP combined with the lower cost of small computers would mean that this would be the standard for scheduling and control even in very small companies.

With the spread of Japanese manufacturing operations on this side of the Pacific in the last decade or so, more and more people got to see and use an alternative to this type of system. This system, often referred to as Kanban, provides material only when it is needed, without the guesswork, so there is never any excess inventory from bad guesses. Now people weren't just reading about something happening in Japan, they were seeing it and using it firsthand.

Kanban

In the Toyota system, each part has its own container designed to hold an exact quantity of that part. There are two Kanban cards for each container. The cards show the part number, the quantity, and any other information that may be necessary.

The first, or production Kanban, is the signal or work order for the work center producing that part. No Kanban, no work. The other serves the next work center in the flow or using work center. Each container cycles from the producing work center and its outgoing stock point to the using work center and its incoming stock point. As the work is done, the kanban cycles back to the producing work center and becomes a work order.

Dual Card Kanban Flows -Machining and Assembly Operation

1. In figure 1 on the following page, find the starting point. Its a full container of machined castings about to be moved to assembly. Its conveyance (C) Kanban is detached and placed in a collection box for stock point A.

2. The container most recently emptied in Assembly is then taken to stock point M where a C Kanban is attached to it.

3. The empty container and C Kanban are taken to stock point M in another area where the C Kanban is taken off and applied to a full container. The full container is taken back to stock point A This triggers production through the use of a production (P) Kanban in the following manner.

4. The full container that just left had a P Kanban attached to it. When it leaves stocking point M its P Kanban is removed and put in a collection box.

5. P Kanban are then taken to Machining every half hour where they go into the dispatch box and become the list of jobs to be worked on next. They are worked on in the order they are received.

6. Completed castings go into an empty container taken from stocking point M The P Kanban is attached and the full container is moved to stocking point M.

Figure 1

Dual Card Kanban Flow

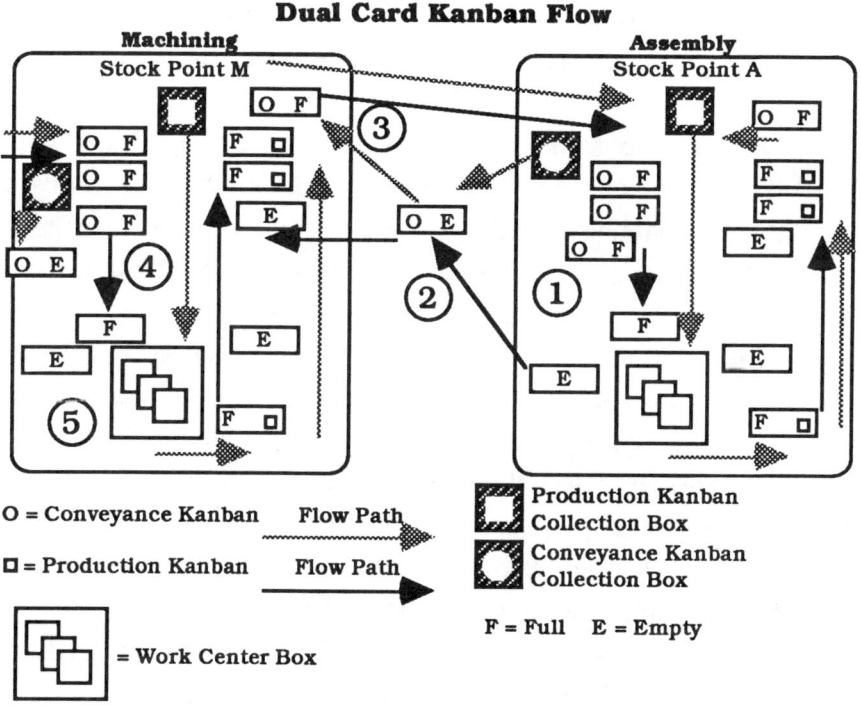

There are a few simple rules that have to be followed to preserve the effectiveness of this system.

First, no castings can be machined unless there is a P Kanban authorizing it. Machining has to come to a halt rather than make castings that are not called for. We are no longer allowing materials to be pushed into areas that are not ready for them.

Secondly, there is one and only one C and P Kanban for each container. The number of containers allowed into the system is the result of a carefully considered management decision. The smaller the number of containers, the smaller the WIP inventory. As with any operating system, there have to be controls and accountability. With this system, there has to be a strict accountability for the Kanbans. Lose any, and you begin to lose control.

Lastly, only standard containers are used. They are always filled with a set exact quantity because with careful control of the amounts in a container and the number of containers in the system, precise inventory control can be maintained without cumbersome manual or expensive computer systems.

Initially the Kanban process could be set up with reasonable buffers built in to take into consideration some of the normal delays and downtime that can occur. As problems are uncovered and corrected this process can be streamlined and sped up very quickly simply by removing one set of C and P Kanbans. If you used five sets and then went to four, that alone would reduce WIP and lead-times through the process by 20%.

The ultimate in efficiency would be one Kanban at each stage of the process but then you have to carefully set up around bottlenecks. Bottlenecks will be addressed separately later.

Single Card Kanban Process - Machining and Assembly Operation

The single card Kanban system has been implemented on a much broader basis than the dual system. The packaging example referred to earlier is an example of such a system. In this system the single card is the conveyance (C) Kanban. It's easier to begin with this system, see how it works, and then add a P Kanban later if that helps the flow and control.

In the single card system, items are produced and purchased according to a regular schedule. Deliveries of material to the user are controlled by the C Kanban. The single card system becomes a small push system for production and a pull system for deliveries.

Figure 2 on the next page shows a single card system for the same Machining and Assembly operation.

1. The beginning point indicated by "start here" starts with a container that has just been emptied. When the container was emptied, the C Kanban was placed in the collection box.

2. When new boxes of material are delivered to the assembly area the C Kanbans are picked up from the collection boxes and delivered to the machining area. The action taken at #2 in this illustration is to attach a C Kanban to a full box of material and deliver it to the assembly work center.

3. Assembly keeps stocking point A supplied with full boxes and keeps producing as long as Kanban signals (C) keep coming.

4. Empty containers are collected regularly from the machining work center and taken to the assembly work center.

This single card system controls deliveries very tightly so the machining area never has more than one or two full containers. The warehouse or picking line servicing the machining area is eliminated and one of the most immediate advantages of this system is the removal of the clutter of the staged boxes around the printing area.

Figure 2

Single Card Kanban Flow

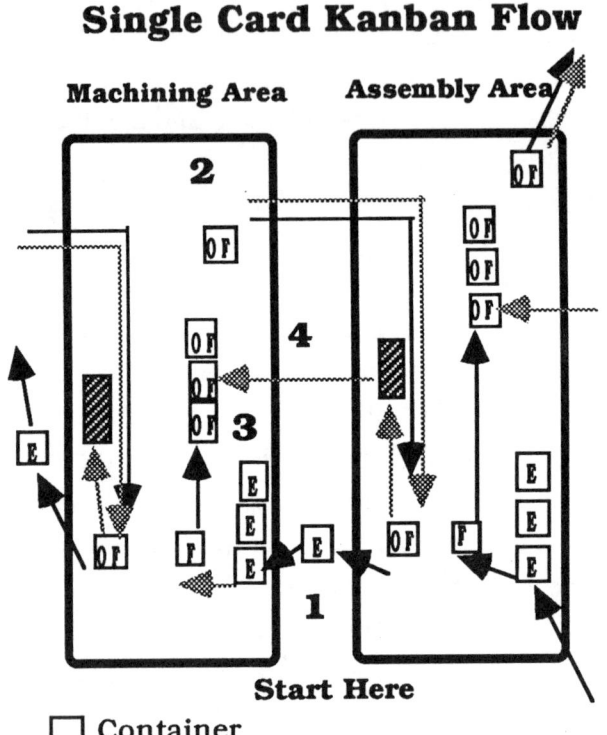

Machining Area   **Assembly Area**

Start Here

☐ Container

O Conveyance (C) Kanban

    E: empty   F: full

▨ Kanban collection box

Material flow path ➡

Kanban flow path ⇢

Cardless Pull System

With a cardless pull system there are no cards to signal production or conveyance activities. Marked staging areas are used instead of Kanbans to control the amount of material in the system. The rule is to run until the downstream staging area is full, then stop. Never push more material downstream than can be stored in that staging area.

After the key work center shuts down for the day, all other work centers in the flow run until their downstream staging areas are full, then shut down. In this manner, the work in process inventory is exactly the same at the end of each day and under tight control. The sizes of the staging areas can be adjusted to increase or decrease the amount of work in process inventory.

Figure three on the next page shows how this system works.

1. The assembly work center empties a full container and it is removed from the staging area.

2. The opening up of a downstream staging area triggers the move of another full container to that area.

3. The removal of a container from stocking point A creates an opening there. That opening is the signal for the machining work center to make one more container.

4. Filling the last container creates the storage space for the empty container that was created in step #1.

5. Careful planning in the sizing of the marked staging areas controls the amount of inventory that can be present in the process.

Figure 3

Cardless Pull System

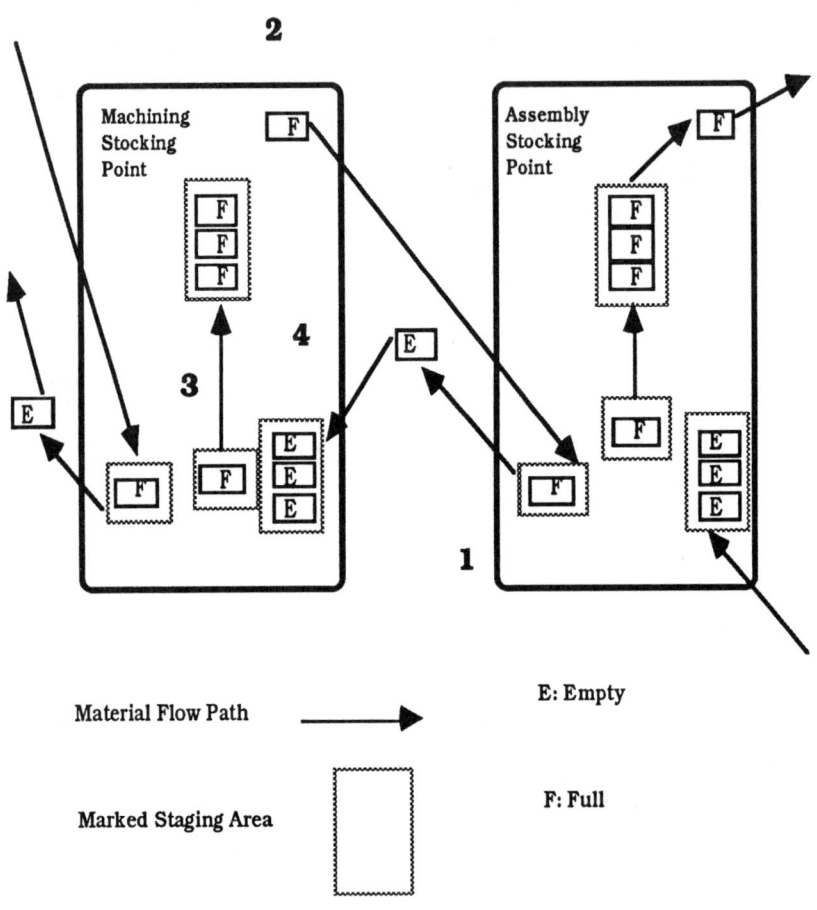

| Material Flow Path | ➡ | E: Empty |
| Marked Staging Area | ▢ | F: Full |

The Demand Pull Game

The last three types of demand pull systems have eliminated much of the wait time in the process. They accomplish this by removing significant amounts of the work in process so once something gets into the system it gets worked on practically right away. It doesn't just get behind some other work. This is one of the key benefits of using this type of shop floor control system over a push system. Other benefits are raising the visibility of quality problems so they can be addressed faster and providing tighter control over inventory.

All three of these benefits:
- reduced throughput time
- tighter inventory control
- greater visibility of problem areas

can be demonstrated clearly in the following type of demonstration.

Push System

Set up a miniature company along two long tables. This company will consist of a four step manufacturing process that will be set up in four stations on the tables. Its product will be paper clip chains of varying length. These chains will be assembled to customer specifications, packaged and marked in an envelope, checked, and shipped.

Continuous Flow

A number of index cards representing orders are marked with numbers from two to twenty five. These numbers are selected at random and it's OK to repeat a number. The smallest number or order we will take is two and the largest is twenty five. For the purposes of this demonstration, we will take no one piece sample orders or any long runs over twenty five.

The numbers represent the length of a paper clip chain on a customer order. The cards are marked and placed face down outside the first step of the demonstration. These will be customer orders. A second number is placed on the card equal to or smaller than the first. This number indicates how many of the first paper clips will be of the larger of two sizes we will be using.

The first station in our little company then will be the order entry process. It is the job of the person at this station to take the top card, assign an order number (recorded on a tablet), record the quantity, create a job jacket by putting the card in an envelope, and mark the job number on the outside of the envelope. When this is done, the envelope is passed down to the next station, production planning.

At this stage, the job jacket is reviewed and assigned a schedule number. The correct number of each size of paper clip is put into the envelope or job jacket and the job is sent into production, the next station.

At the third, or production station, the job jacket is opened, instructions read, and the paper clip chain is assembled according to these instructions. The chain is put back into the job jacket and sent down to the last station, inspect and ship.

At the last station, the chain is removed and inspected. If it is correct it gets put in a separate shipping envelope, the job number is marked on both sides, and the order is shipped. If the chain is assembled incorrectly, it is sent back to production planning to be scheduled for rework.

It takes about thirty minutes or so to run this demonstration effectively. Before you get started you will need enough index cards, envelopes, paper clips, and shipping envelopes to run this long and you will need a marking board to record how these processes will be measured.

Start the demonstration and make sure everyone understands their job. Let it run for at least five minutes. At this point it will become apparrent that jobs will be piling up in one or two areas.

After about five minutes, introduce a smaller clip size at the planning station. The planner is to put the smaller clip in the envelope and the assembler is to assemble them. This is to simulate an undetected defect getting into the process. When these parts get to the inspection part of the process and are detected, stop the line. Count up the work in process inventory that has to be gone through to sort out the small clips and record that on the board under the WIP column.

Correct the quality problem and start the line up for about another five minutes again. At this time, ask someone else to play the part of a customer service representative and ask them to find a certain (any) job number and report back on how many large clips are in that job. On the marking board, record the amount of time this takes.

Lastly, while the operation is running, insert a colored job jacket into the front of the line at order entry and record how much time it takes to get it all the way through and out through shipping.

Continuous Flow

Another measure you may want to include is the amount of time that elapsed between the introduction of a poor quality product to the line and its discovery. When you have completed this push portion of the demonstration you will have a leadtime or throughput time, a typical work in process inventory level, and an idea of how long it takes to discover a quality problem, and an idea of how long it takes to locate and check on a job in this little company.

Pull System

Now clear off the tables and get ready to run this same company with a pull system instead. This will be modeled after the no card system just covered. Tape about a twelve inch square to the left of each work station as the people are facing the stations. The flow will be from their right, through their station, and into the square to their left. The only thing different they will be doing in this new set up from the previous push example is they will have adopted a very simple rule. They can only put one job into the square on their left and they can only do that when the square is empty. If that square is full, they cannot pull any more work into their work station, they must stop.

Start the process up again and let run for a few minutes. It soon becomes apparent from the waiting time at some of the stations that the work is not balanced. In a real world situation these would be opportunities for job consolidations and other cost reduction activities.

60

Introduce the small, bad quality paper clips in the same manner as the first run. Stop the line when they are discovered in shipping and record the elapsed time between the introduction of the bad clips and their discovery. Also record the work in process inventory that had to be gone through to correct the problem.

When this is completed start the line up again and let it run for a few more minutes. Have someone do the customer service bit again on a job in the system and record how long it takes to find the job.

Finally, send the colored job jacket through the system and record how long the new throughput time is.

When you have completed both versions of how to run this little factory you will have observed both a push system and a pull system doing the same identical tasks. By now some of the advantages of a pull system should be very apparent if you took the trouble to actually do this exercise and not just read about it.

From the information recorded on the board during the demonstration you will have observed four important benefits that the pull system has over the more traditional push system.

1. Typically the work in process inventory levels that have to be sorted through when there is a quality problem are significantly lower with the pull system.

2. Quality problems are not hidden as with the push system. The awareness of the problems and the response to them is much more immediate.

3. The customer service response time part of this role play showed just how much easier to find things and hence, control them in this system. It doesn't have to be customer service as in

this situation. If everyone has an easier time getting immediate access to what is in the flow, the overall level of control will rise.

4. The throughput time for the whole process is reduced dramatically. As in the highway example, there are no cars on the road so there is no rush hour. This translates to reduced lead times.

The Effect of Bottlenecks

One dimension that was not measured during this demonstration was the total output of this company over the time elapsed or the amount of throughput. In the just in time example, all stations are shut down if their squares are full. If there is an operation that is slower than the rest that has a lot of demand on it, this stopping is hurting the throughput. So on one hand we get hurt if we let things run on their own and on the other hand we can choke our throughput if we blindly follow the dictates of a pure pull system. What's the solution?

Lets go back to our car on the highway example. Did you ever notice that when you go on a long trip with a group of cars that it doesn't take very long before the cars in back have to do a lot of speeding from time to time just to keep up? They stop at a rest area and get all over the lead driver for going too fast and making it hard for them to keep up.

Not only that , one of the cars in the middle of the pack is driven by a very conservative driver and once it falls behind it can never go fast enough to catch up much to the chagrin of those stuck behind that car.

The lead drivers will swear that they never went over fifty five miles per hour and the drivers in the very back will swear they had to do seventy five miles per hour from time to time to catch up. If both of them are telling the truth, and they are, what is going on?

There are two things happening in this type of situation. There is the effect that normal statistical variation can have on this line of cars and there is the effect that the slow car can have on the line. If your objective is to get from city A to city B in the shortest amount of time your key measurement is the time it takes the last car to get there in terms of throughput time.

For control in insuring that no-one gets lost, the main concern will be the distance between the first and last car.

Normal statistical fluctuations can affect the spacing among the cars in the following manner.

If the rule is you can't pass the car in front of you you will all slow down for a deer crossing the road if it happens to pass in front of the lead car. If it comes between the lead car and the second car, the lead car pulls away and all the other cars have to speed up to catch up. If the second car is the slowest car this problem gets worse because not only is there a gap between the main car and the rest of the cars, the slowness of the second car is keeping that gap from closing up.

Have this random type of interference happen enough and pretty soon the cars are strung out all over the place.

A partial solution here is to have the slower car become the lead car. This is akin to the pioneers practice of having the slowest wagon lead the wagon train. You still experience the normal stretching and contractions as the cars have to slow down for different reasons   but now they are not held back in their own ability to catch up by someone slower than they are in front of them, so eventually they will catch up to the slow car.

The lead car never slows down for reasons affecting the other cars. Now if it is the lead car and the deer crosses the road behind it it is able to keep going. Since it is no longer in the way of the other cars trying to close the distance, they will catch up.

Now it will slow down or stop for conditions affecting it alone. Changing its position in the line has in effect insulated or buffered it from having to slow down for reasons associated with the other cars.

In manufacturing, we call those slow cars **bottlenecks.** To use a pure Kanban system on a flow involving a bottleneck, we would have to move the bottleneck down to the last operation using the car fix as an example.

Since that cannot be done most of the time, the problem becomes one of insulating the bottleneck from the normal statistical fluctuations that can affect the rest of the line. We don't want the bottleneck to shut down for any of the reasons associated with the other work stations.

In our little company, the bottleneck was the paper clip assembly operation. The following continuation of this demonstration illustrates how a bottleneck in the middle of a line flow can be buffered.

Pull System With Buffers

Set the demonstration company back up on the table just as before. Have the squares marked just as in the second just in time version. This time run the demonstration for exactly ten minutes. As part of this ten minutes, shut the shipping operation down for three minutes because they ran out of packaging. When the demonstration is over, total up the amount of throughput that came off the line.

It is best for the purpose of this demonstration to have the out of stock situation occur during the middle of this time frame. Record the throughput on the marking board.

Now set all the stations back up again with one simple modification. Enlarge the square downstream from the bottleneck so it can hold five jobs. All the other squares in the line remain the same but the rule is modified for the bottleneck so it can keep producing up to five jobs should the line downstream stop for any reason.

Start the demonstration and run it with this modification. The total elapsed time should be exactly the same as the first run since we will be comparing output over time. Include the same three minutes of downtime for shipping to run out of packaging (envelopes). For the basis of comparison, this downtime should occur at the same time during the run. After time is up, record the total throughput on the board.

What you will see is that a slight modification in the square size for the bottleneck allowed for an increased amount of throughput over the same time. We have created the same effect of moving the slow car to the head of the line so it can keep moving even though the other operations have stopped. We maximize the uptime of the botleneck so we can get the most out of it and we still have much tighter control over the inventory than with the push system.

Continuous Flow

You can time the throughput and see an increase over the pure pull system example but it is still better than the push system. An additional buffer upstream of the bottleneck could be considered to protect it from running out of material when they shut down.

Obstacles to Implementation

Going to a just in time or pull production system will smooth the flow of materials through an operation and buffering the bottlenecks will make sure that flow is as fast as practical. The fact that very few organizations have been able to make much progress in this area in spite of tremendous expenditures of money, time, and effort seems to be traced back to two general causes.

1 Many managers do not have enough insight, experience, or education to have a clear vision of how to achieve this type of product flow in an ever changing, complicated, and dynamic environment.

2. There is a sharp conflict between the measurements required for a smooth continuous flow and existing management accounting practices.

Outdated cost accounting approaches to measurement make it difficult to identify and control the constraints that exist in every company. Constraints are a larger and more strategic version of the bottlenecks we were just looking at.

Constraints

If a company didn't have any constraints it would be making an unlimited amount of money so when you think of it, every organization has at least one. Simply put, a constraint is any element of the company that keeps it from making more money.

These constraints can shift around depending upon the circumstances so for management to improve the productivity and profitability of the company, they must focus on the constraints that are limiting performance. The good news is there aren't usually many of them   but since they are likely to shift over time, you have to be sure you're dealing with the correct one. If you didn't, you may find yourself planning for the last war rather than the next one.

Most are aware how material and capacity problems can constrain a process   but are unaware that market, behavioral, logistical, and managerial constraints also exist and are often unrecognized as constraints with their disruptions attributed to material or capacity problems.

Material Constraints

Without the materials to do the job, the company shuts down. The need to keep large amounts of materials on hand is a necessity derived from this fact. Poor material control practices that contribute to oversupplies or stock outages can create more problems than they solve.

Continuous Flow

There are short term material constraints such as a supplier missing a delivery schedule or a bad lot of material is recieved. Using a forecast with a short time horizon   when purchasing materials with long lead times will also make problems inevitable. Long term material constraints are more strategic involving broad based shortages. The impact the oil shortages had on the petrochemical industry is an example.

Material constraints can also develop in the manufacturing process itself whenever there is insufficient work in process inventory. These problems are usually traced to one of five causes.

1. Material shortages are often the result of poor scheduling of the product flow. The use of a Kanban system is usually effective here.

2. Material can be damaged in transit by an inadequate material conveyance system.

3. An operation can produce so much scrap that cannot be reworked as to use up all the material available.

4. A feeder station upstream has unscheduled downtime therby starving the downstream operations of materials.

5. Material for one order can be diverted to another creating a material shortage for the order in question.

Capacity Constraints

A capacity constraint exists when the available capacity at a work center is insufficient to support the current throughput demands. When this happens, the potential product flow through the organization is disrupted. When one thinks of constraints, capacity constraints are the first that come to mind because they are common, and easy to identify.

In our flow demonstration, we made the distinction between bottleneck and non-bottleneck resources. A non-bottleneck resource had a capacity that was greater than any demand placed on it. The bottleneck resoure was the one that couldn't keep up because its capacity was less than the demand placed on it. If there are bottlenecks in the flow, that flow will be less than desired until the capacity of any bottleneck is increased.

A temporary bottleneck is a resource that restricts the flow some times and at later times can have plenty of capacity. This becomes readily apparent in a seasonal operation.

When a bottleneck exists, throughput is jeapordized. It can be lost, and due dates can be missed due to lack of processing capacity of one or more work centers.

Even in operations that have no true bottlenecks, there can be one or more resources that have the potential to totally disrupt the product flow. These are called **capacity constraint resources (CCR's)**

A capacity constraint resource is a resource likely to cause the flow of product through the process to deviate from plan unless it is properly scheduled and managed. A capacity constraint resource can be either a bottleneck or a non-bottleneck resource.

We will use the following illustration to clarify this concept.

In a company described in the following table, consoles and keyboard covers are manufactured by processing them through the administrative, production planning, Tooling, and production resources in that sequence. Demand averages 20 consoles and 50 keyboard covers per day. The resource capacity to support that demand level is 23 hours of administration, 24 hours of production planning, 31 hours of tooling, and 7 hours of production. There are only 24 hours in a day so by definition, the production planning and Tooling resources are bottlenecks since their processing time requirements are less than the current demand.

Now let's see if any of these resources are capacity constraining resources, likely to disrupt the flow if not properly managed. Looking at the bottlenecks first, we see that the flow is controlled by the most severe bottleneck and not usually by the others. In this example, the flow of orders through production planning is constrained by the fact that Tooling is processing jobs at a slower rate. As long as this is the case, then production planning does not directly cotrol the flow of jobs through the process. If there is a backup, it will be in Tooling.

Since Tooling has the greatest capacity requirement and it exceeds available capacity, it is the primary constraint on the flow of orders. Therefore, any mismanagement in Tooling that results in lost processing time causes a reduction in sales throughput for the company and may adversely affect on time delivery performance. Even though production planning is a bottleneck in this example, it is not an active constraint on the process and need not be considered when planning the product flow.

Tooling is the resource that has to be watched so it is a capacity constraining resource where production planning is not.

Now one very large order can change everything around to where production can now become the capacity constraining resource.

Demonstrating relationships between capacity constraint resources (CCR's) and non CCR's

Hours of Resource Time Required to Produce one Average Job.

Average Demand per 24 hr day		Admin	Planning	Tooling	Production
		A	Pl	T	Pr
Consoles	20 Jobs	.8	.2	.3	.2
Covers	50 Jobs	.1	.4	.5	.1

Required and Available Capacity

	A	Pl	T	Pr
Required Capacity per Day	21	24	31	9
Available Capacity per Day	24	24	24	24

Logistical Constraints

A logistical constraint is any constraint that is inherent in the operations planning and control system used by the company. This constraint impedes the smooth flow of orders through the system. They can affect the flow at any point from order entry through shipping. They are built into the system and are difficult to change. In many cases they are not even recognized by managers as something that can be improved on. For example.................."The System says......." However, if the constraints imposed by the system are too difficult to work with and significantly disrupt the process, the system must be modified or changed.

For example, imagine an order processing system that uses order entry from the field sales force, customer calls, faxes, and orders mailed in. Orders are collected and forwarded to the order entry department where they are combined, assigned a ship date, and entered into the system. During a busy season this activity is much higher than the capacity of the department during the beginning of the week, then tapers off towards the end of the week allowing them to catch up.

Such a process may, at times, require a few days to get these orders into the system. The eventual lead time to the customer will be delayed by the length of the order processing lead time.

Another illustration would be the use of week of ship dates. By using time frames of one week duration instead of discrete daily increments there is a loss of visibility of the exact due dates for the orders. This means for every order to be on time, some will be almost a week early. In addition, the total lead time will be needlessly increased depending on the actual operating system.

These then would be examples of logistical constraints that people don't generally think to look at that can be impeding the smooth flow of product or orders through the system.

Management Constraints

Management constraints are the strategics, policies, and practices that can act as a damper on operations related decisions. In most cases, these constraints are the result of a lack of understanding of the factors that can improve or impede a smooth flowing operation.

There are two basic ways these constraints can affect the system. They can create situations that suboptimize the process or they can compound the effect that other constraints can have on the system.

For example, consider a company that awards its sourcing people based on their ability to secure a low price on the products purchased. If that company did not have a full understanding of the problems that poor quality raw material could create through each step of the job flow it is very probable that any initial savings could be wiped out a few times over by the effects of any poor quality.

Management constraints can also have the effect of aggravating the problems caused by other constraints. An example is the practice of letting people independently sequence jobs at non-bottleneck operations in order to speed up their output. Given the existence of bottlenecks in the system, the poor overall schedules typically generated by this policy will likely disrupt the smooth flow of the overall system. As a result, throughput for the company as a whole   could be lost, lead times extended, and on time delivery could suffer.

Behavioral Constraints

Companies are often remembered by the attitudes of their workforce. To the degree that habits are developed and practiced that run contrary to the principles of a smooth running organization, these practices become a constraint on the system. They become an attitude that reflects the culture of the entire organization.

In most environments they evolve as a result of a mangagement style practiced in concert with the financial reward system. Therefore, management may be at least partially responsible for many of the behavioral constraints.

An example of a behavioral constraint is a "look busy" attitude. This attitude may have its origins in the fear that people who aren't busy won't be around in the future. As an example, to the extent that a foundry has excess capacity, the result of this frame of mind could be castings that are prepared but not needed or required. This practice does not add to the throughput of the company. It only generates an excessive number of jobs in progress that dilute control and bring on longer lead times.

Another example of a behavioral constraint is the tendency for operators to cherry pick the jobs waiting to be run. Everyone wants to look good and by picking the easy jobs they get to have a good day with all the respect and good feelings that go along with it.

This practice causes the best jobs to run first leaving the rest to run later. Best in the eyes of the operator, not the overall system. This practice can destroy a schedule and cause missed deliveries.

When they exist, behavioral constraints are often very difficult to remove because they are so deeply rooted. This difficulty makes them a major obstacle to a continuous flow process.

Obstacles to Constraint Management

Identifying and controlling all of the constraints of an operating company is a virtual impossibility. As soon as constraints are identified and brought under control, new constraints pop up in other areas. The process of constraint management never ends. Remember, if there were no constraints, the company would be making an unlimited amount of money.

No matter how well events are planned, the actual flow will differ from that plan. This is due to these three factors.

1. Unpredictable stoppages occur. Even though you may have an excellent history of average downtimes for every reason, you cannot predict when the next random stoppage will occur.

2. Inaccurate information or information that cannot be determined in advance. Again, you may know the average time to

run an order but you cannot predict the exact time for each order in advance.

3. Large numbers of other variables. Each work center is influenced by such a large number of variables that they are not all considered in the planning process.

As a result, the actual production flow, when examined in detail, will not match the planned flow. All of the various constraints just mentioned will interact in such a way as to disrupt that flow.

A pull system management philosophy can be utilized to minimize the adverse effects generated by constraints.

In general, the most important task a manager faces is to continuously remove constraints that are getting in the way of the company's ability to remain profitable.

Reducing Constraint Influence

Now that you have somewhat of an understanding of what the various constraints are, here is a simple six step method for improving the system by reducing their influence.

1. Identify the constraints in the process.

2. Determine what has to be done to exploit the constraints and improve performance

3. Place your emphasis on the constraints, not the other parts of the process.

4. Execute whatever steps that are identified that would improve the performance of the process.

5. If, in doing the above, a constraint has been removed or a new one identified, go back to step # 1.

6. Measure the progress using throughput measurements, not traditional accounting measures.

In summarizing this review of constraints, they exist in every organization and limit the ability of the company to improve productivity and make more money. They can appear in many forms. Sometimes it's the market that is the major limitation on what the company can achieve. Material and capacity constraints place physical limitations on what the company can produce. Management, logistical, and behavioral constraints bring inefficiencies into the company and may also aggravate the problems caused by the other constraints.

It becomes apparent that some excess capacity which would be considered expensive and undesirable under the old cost measurement systems is very desirable in helping to manage constraints.

Implementation

Implementing a continuous flow strategy can produce fast results in most operating environments because it sharpens the focus on the common goal of the company. Every new product, every activity, and every decision is evaluated in terms of whether it contributes to the common company wide goal. Three important elements are necessary to implement continuous flow.

Continuous Flow

1. Define the common goal of the company in meaningful terms that can be easily understood. Example: Make money now and in the future. Continuous flow brings a new set of operational measures that define this common goal. These are measures of throughput, inventory, and operating expense. They are universally acceptable because they can be applied to any manufacturing company across the entire scope of the economy. By shifting emphasis from traditional localized measures, it is possible for everyone to relate to one common goal.

2. Develop the causal relationship between individual actions and the common goal. Continuous flow establishes a set of principles that enable the use of throughput, inventory, and operating expense measures to relate specific operating actions to the enhancement of the common goal. Some of these principles can be used in alternative marketing and operating strategies in terms of their impact on overall throughput, inventory, and operating expense.

They can also be used to establish appropriate material and production control systems that will be necessary to improve the peformance of the company with respect to these measures.

3. Manage the various actions as to achieve the greatest benefit. Continuous flow is the basis for material and production control system changes in a complex operating environment. This includes procedures for identifying and managing all the constraints of the system and for providing a framework for continuous improvement. To analyze an entire operation effectively, all company constraints; -- Market, Capacity, Material, Logistical, Management, and Behavioral must be identified.

Then, with a focused analysis, appropriate policies and procedures can be designed and developed to provide for the continuous flow of the company.

Any current policies and procedures likely to conflict with improving overall company competitiveness can also be eliminated or modified.

The continuous flow philosophy allows everyone to focus in on those areas that are offering the greatest opportunity for total company improvement. This global focused improvement becomes a catalyst in a program of company wide continuous improvement.

Once you have these elements in place, you will have an all encompassing operating philosophy that includes an appropriate set of policies and procedures where every action is evaluated in terms of the common company wide goal.

These principles can be applied to any organization.

Controlling the

Business

*There is always an easy solution to every human problem
-neat, plausible, and wrong.*

H. L. Mencken

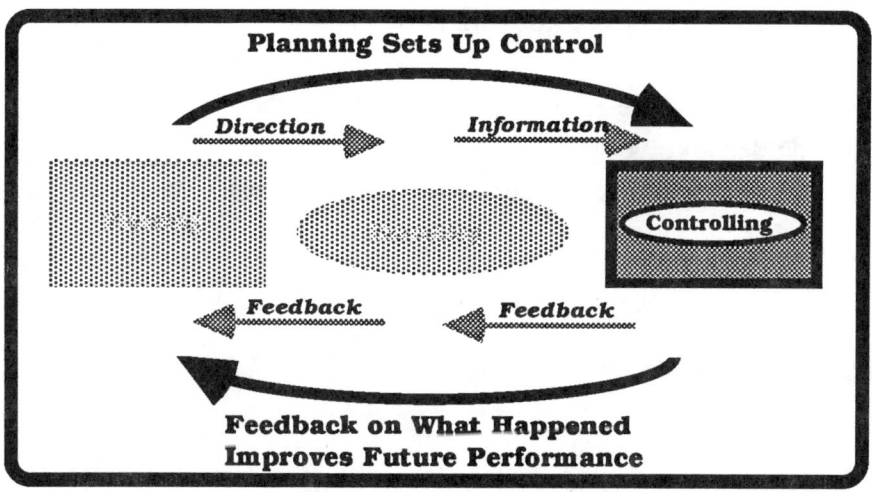

Introduction to Statistical Process Control

There are two and only two mistakes you can make in managing a process. You can leave a situation alone that needs attending to or you can tend to a situation that should be left alone. The use of statistically valid signals to increase your "odds" of making the correct decision is known as **Statistical Process Control**. What follows is an outline of how to set up and use those signals.

The greatest barrier to the implementation of statistical process control throughout an organization is the mistaken idea that the concepts are too difficult for the average person to understand.

Now, there is no question that the theory on which it is based does involve some high level mathematics;

For example, the normal probability density function:

$$f(y) \;=\; \frac{e^{-(y-\mu)^2/2\sigma^2}}{\sigma\sqrt{2\pi}}, (-\infty \langle y \langle +\infty)$$

The symbols e and π represent irrational numbers whose values are approximately 2.7183 and 3.1416 respectively while μ and σ are the population mean and standard deviation. The equation for the density function is constructed such that the area under the curve will represent probability so the total area is equal to one.

As complicated as this looks, you don't have to be a long haired mathematician to use these statistical methods.

Variation

Anyone who has ever spent time with kids can attest to the fact that there is an awareness of statistical variation that comes to children at an early age. If you ever have any doubts about this, put a plate of brownies in front of a few of them and stand back and watch the arguing over who gets the biggest one and who gets stuck with the smallest one.

This shows an understanding of one of the essentials of statistics. **There is variation in everything that can be found if you have a method of measurement that is sensitive enough to detect that variation.** No two castings, cans, nails, or boxes are exactly the same. Even though two items may look alike, when seen through a microscope, they are very different. We call these differences **variation**.

The Normal Curve

Now, on second thought, how did those kids know which was the largest brownie? Actually its probably pretty easy to find the biggest and the smallest but it would be very difficult to arrange the entire plate by size order.

To do that we would have to weigh each one down to the nearest gram on a very accurate and sensitive scale. If we weighed a hundred of these brownies, here's what we would find.

Histogram of 100 Brownies by Size

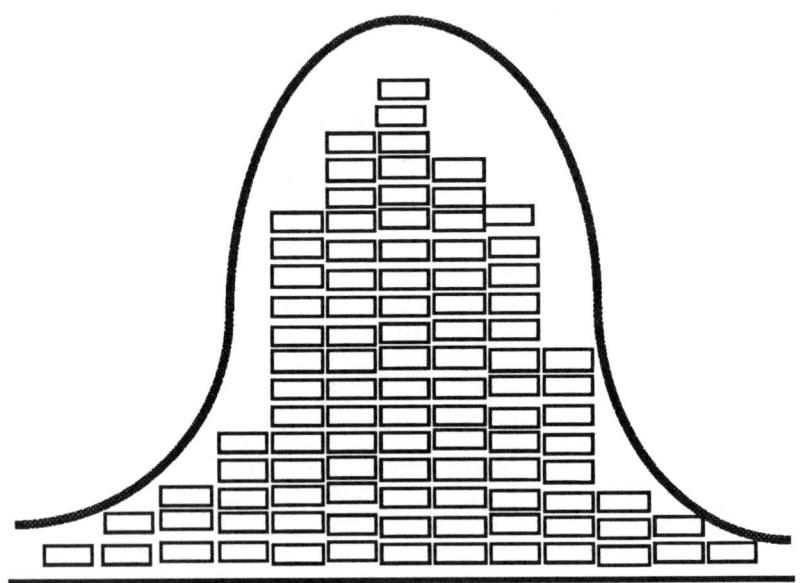

Just as we suspected, we were correct in there being big and small brownies. What we also see is that the number of brownies in each gram step varies from the smallest to the largest in a fairly regular and bell shaped pattern. This pattern was so regular that we were able to draw a smooth curve over the plots that very closely fits the distribution.

If we did this measuring process over and over we would find a very similar pattern in plotting each group.

This pattern repeats itself over and over again, not only in brownies, but in apples, caps, baseballs, and any manufactured articles.

We could look at thousands of patterns like this. The measurements might be in length, degrees Fahrenheit, calls answered per day, or ounces per square inch. Though there might be all kinds of different measurements, there will always be an inherent variability in those measurements that can be measured if the detecting instrument is sensitive enough to measure those variations.

These variations usually follow the same bell shaped pattern that we call the **normal curve.**

Parameters of the Normal Curve

For example:

The average inside diameter of a coffee mug imported from Indonesia is 2.832 inches. Individual mugs can vary in size from 2.8 inches to 2.87 inches. Sixty eight percent are between 2.82 inches and 2.84 inches and ninety-five percent are between 2.809 inches and 2.854 inches.

You would very seldom see a coffee mug with an inside diameter greater then 2.87 inches. All of this information came from the following two numbers.

$$\overline{X} \;=\; 2.832$$

$$\sigma \;=\; .01141$$

The first number, $\overline{X}$, tells us that the **average** inside diameter is 2.832 inches. That's the center of this normal curve where we find the largest percentage of mugs.

This number is pronounced ex bar.

The second number is indicated by σ which is the greek letter sigma. It is known as the **standard deviation.**

For those who relish this sort of thing, it is arrived at by taking the positive square root of the **variance** σ^2 where:

$$S'^2 \;=\; \frac{\sum\limits_{i=1}^{n} (y_i - \overline{y})^2}{n}$$

where n is the number of each (y) measurement.

In technical terms, this formula determines the distance from the center of the distribution where the curve stops curving downward and deviates to start curving outward.

Probability and the Area Under the Curve

By knowing about the mathematics, we can use $\overline{X}$ and σ in the formulas for the normal curve shown earlier and can compute the number of mugs between any two dimensions we may want to investigate.

For most of our purposes, however, we're going to be mainly interested in the points at one, two, and three standard deviations on either side of the center.

If we go out one standard deviation from each side of the center of our mug curve, sixty-eight percent of the area under the curve will be between the lines drawn through those two points.

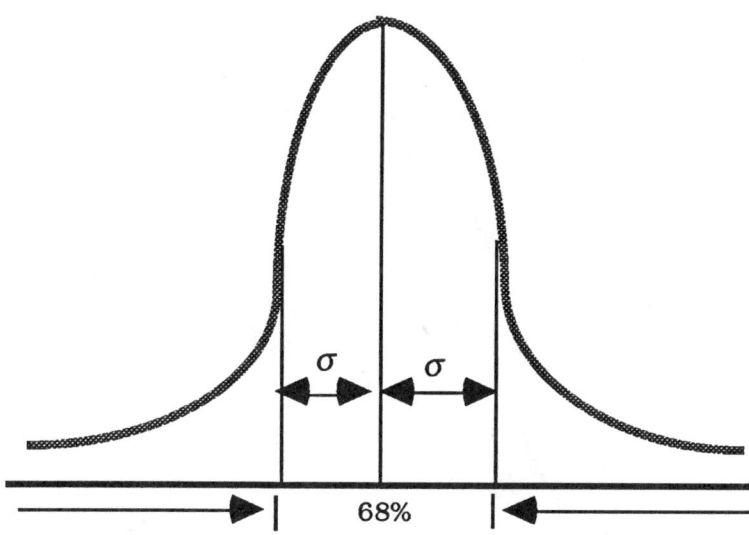

Two standard deviations would be .0228 inches, so ninety-five percent of the mugs would have inside diameters between 2.809 inches and 2.854 inches.

$$\sigma = .01141$$
$$\underline{X \quad 2}$$
$$.0228$$

2.832 - .0228 = 2.809"
2.832 + .0228 = 2.854"

Three standard deviations are .0342 inches. Since 99.73 percent of the area under the normal curve is between minus three sigma (σ) and plus three sigma we can say that just about all these mugs have inside dimensions between 2.80 inches and 2.87 inches.

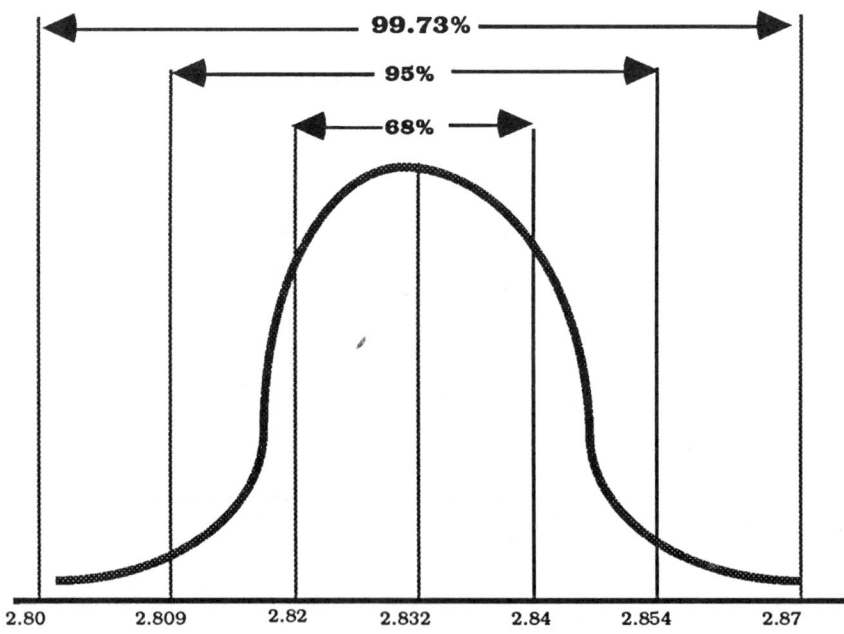

Since we didn't account for all the mugs (99.73%), we can say that there will be a few above 2.87" but they will amount to about thirteen in ten thousand. About the same number will be below 2.8".

Now what we have to do is take all this and understand how it can be applied to just about everything, not just coffee mugs and brownies. This is where we get into something called **probability**.

Suppose we went down to the receiving dock where we could measure the inside diameter of every coffee mug coming into the building. What odds would you give that a mug would be exactly 2.832" wide? That is the average you know.

Since we already know that the mug could be anywhere from 2.80 to 2.87 inches in diameter you would have to give pretty big odds that one would be exactly 2.832".

Suppose then we said that the next coffee mug had to be between 2.82" and 2.84". How would we figure the odds?

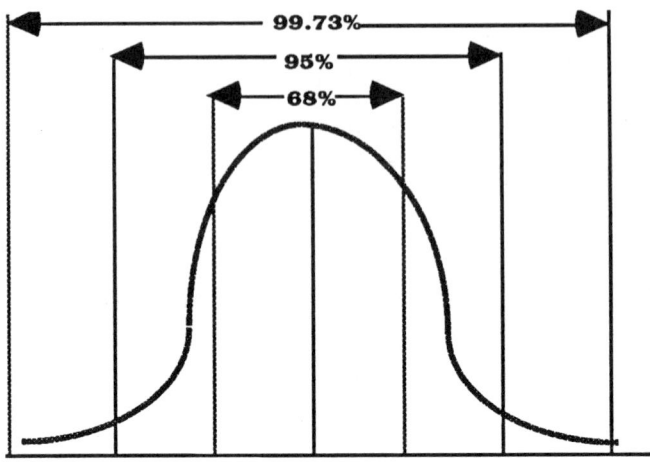

We have already seen the answer to that. Sixty-eight percent of all coffee mugs are between 2.82" and 2.84". That means there are sixty eight chances in one hundred that the next coffee mug would be between those two limits. We would have to give odds of sixty eight to thirty two (100 less 68), or just about two to one.

Ninety-five percent of all coffee mugs are between 2.809" and 2.854", so the odds are ninety-five to five, or 19 to 1 that the next coffee mug won't be smaller than 2.809" or larger than 2.854".

Since there are five chances in one hundred that a mug will be smaller or larger than 2.809" or 2.854", there must be only two and one half chances in one hundred that a mug will be larger than 2.854" and thirteen and one half chances in ten thousand or one in seven hundred forty (10,000/ 13.5 = 740.74) that a mug will be larger than 2.87"

Using Probability in a Molding Shop

Let's put this in a business sense. We want to make a molded cup lid that has to fit properly into the cup. We know from experience that when the part weighs exactly ten grams we have the best fit between the cup and the lid. We want each lid to weigh as close to ten grams as possible.

We have a special molding machine that will mold these lids. We measured a lot of five hundred that was run yesterday and here's what we found.

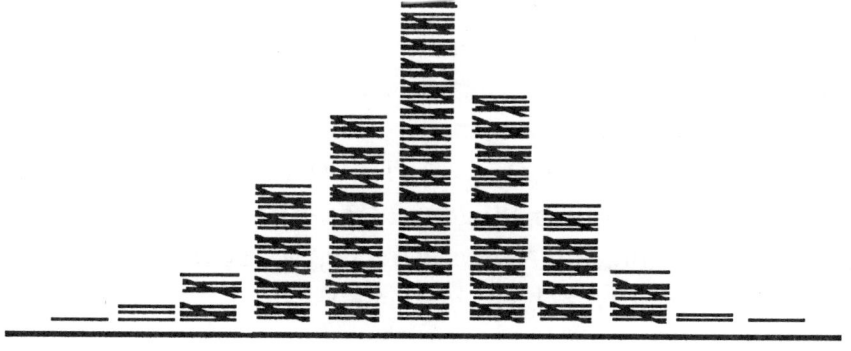

This is called a **histogram** or **fequency distribution**.

Again, we see the familiar pattern of the normal curve as we saw with the brownies and the coffee mugs.

The average is ten grams and the variation means they can be as small as 9.55 grams or as large as 10.45 grams. For our use they are acceptable for we know we have a tolerance of ten grams plus or minus .75 grams.

This is known as a **specification limit** or spec limit and means that anything that falls between 9.25 grams and 10.75 grams is acceptable as it falls within the specification limits.

Our problem is to keep the machine at the center of ten grams and not let the individual lids vary much more than they did in this lot.

All of these lids were made at the same time, by the same operator, and from the same batch of raw material so we could conclude that the pattern of this variation would fit the usual normal curve.

We also know that the greatest size variance we would find would be about minus three and plus three standard deviations or a spread of six standard deviations.

The difference between the largest at 10.45 grams and the smallest at 9.55 grams is .90 grams. One sixth of .90 grams is .15 grams so in using this crude estimate, we could say that the standard deviation was about .15 grams.

The Use of Sampling

There is a shorter way to get information that is just about as valuable without having to measure all five hundred lids. You can pick out a **sample** of five lids at random and record the results. For this to work, the sample lids have to be selected from all parts of the production run at random.

We do this until we have five samples of five lids and plot the results like this.

Sample	1	2	3	4	5	
	9.925	10.125	10.010	9.865	10.165	
	9.770	9.815	9.940	10.230	10.015	
	10.080	10.075	9.995	9.705	10.185	
	10.135	10.295	9.980	10.005	9.840	
	9.700	9.950	9.890	10.045	10.065	Grand Average
Average	9.975	10.052	9.963	9.970	10.054	10.003
Range	.365	.48	.12	.525	.0345	.367

These five sample averages vary quite a bit from the lot average of ten grams, but the average of the sample averages is 10.005 grams. We won't always come as close to the actual average of the lot of five hundred in five samples but if we have enough samples, say over twenty, the average of a number of samples can be used to approximate the actual average of the lot.

In the lot of five hundred lids, we divided the difference between the largest and smallest by six to get our estimate of the standard deviation. We can't do this in samples of only five. Earlier we had five hundred chances of getting some of the extreme values. Since the chances of that happening are much smaller for samples of five, we have to use a small divisor as well.

This divisor is called the d_2 factor and its value for sample sizes of two to ten can be found in the last column of the following table.

Tables of Constants for Variables Control Charts
$\overline{X}$ & r Control Charts

Sample Size n	A_2	D_3	D_4	d_2
2	1,880	-	3.267	1.128
3	1.023	-	2.574	1.693
4	0.729	-	2.282	2.059
5	0.577	-	2.114	2.325
6	0.483	-	2.004	2.534
7	0.419	0.076	1.924	2.704
8	0.373	0.136	1.864	2.847
9	0.337	0.184	1.816	2.970
10	0.308	0.223	1.777	3.078

$\overline{X}$ & s Control Charts

Sample Size n	A_3	B_3	B_4	c_4
2	2.659	-	3.267	.7979
3	1.954	-	2.568	.8862
4	1.628	-	2.266	.9213
5	1.427	-	2.089	.9400
6	1.287	0.030	1.970	.9515
7	1.182	0.118	1.882	.9594
8	1.099	0.185	1.815	.9650
9	1.032	0.239	1.761	.9693
10	0.975	0.284	1.716	.9727

For a sample of five, the d_2 factor is 2.326. Dividing the average range, .3679 by 2.326 gives us a standard deviation of .158

which is very close to the .150 figure we got after measuring five hundred lids.

This is a good demonstration of the fact that a few samples can be used to effectively estimate the two most important aspects of the distribution of the measurements of any product.

They are the **average,** $\overline{X}$, and the **standard deviation** σ. The standard deviation is normally refereed to by its Greek name, Sigma.

The sigma of our lids is .15 grams and the average is ten grams. With these two values we can now put some percentage figure on the distribution which is the normal curve.

If the process is centered on the average of ten grams, 68% should be between 9.85 grams and 10.15 grams. The space between minus 2 sigma and plus 2 sigma, or between 9.79 grams and 10.39 grams will give us 95% of the values. Plus or minus three sigma or between 9.55 grams and 10.45 grams should give us 99.73% of the lids.

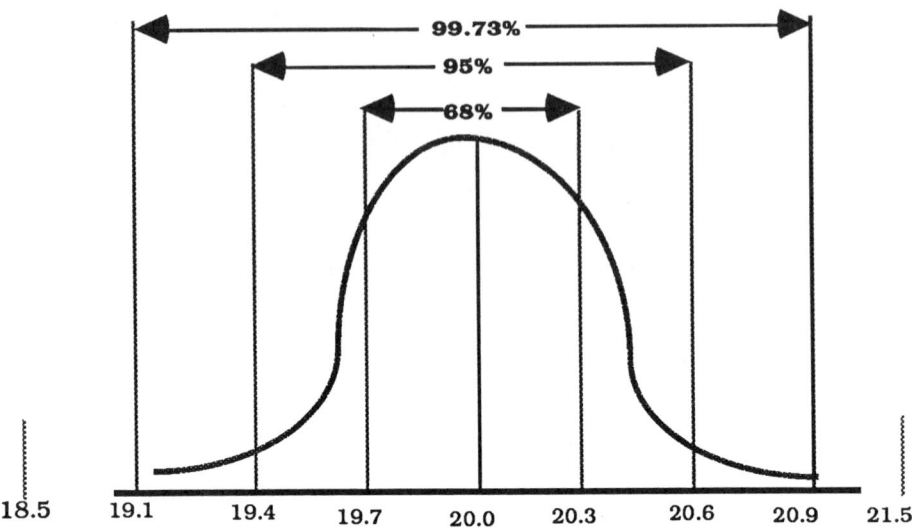

$$\overline{X} \pm 1\sigma \qquad \overline{X} \pm 2\sigma \qquad \overline{X} \pm 3\sigma$$

$\overline{X} \pm 1\sigma$	$\overline{X} \pm 2\sigma$	$\overline{X} \pm 3\sigma$
(20.0+.3= 20.3)	(20.0+.6= 20.6)	(20.0+.9= 20.9)
(20.0- .3= 19.7)	(20.0- .6= 19.4)	(20.0- .9= 19.1)
68%	95%	99.73%

Even if something irregular happened to give us an occasional lid that was lighter than 9.55 grams or heavier than 10.45 grams, as long as the molding machine is properly set to make an average of ten grams, we could give odds of 997 to 3 or 332 to one that you couldn't walk out into the shop and pick out a lid at random that would be outside these limits.

But, we all know that our processes don't always do what they are supposed to do.

Let's take what happened yesterday for example. One of our operators must have had a lot on her mind because it certainly wasn't focused on making lids. Yesterday her machine setting was off about two tenths of a gram.

How do we know this? We take a look at the shape of the distribution of the lids produced on that shift.

Her average was 10.2 grams. The pattern of the variation of the individual measurements about the center of 10.2 grams was the same as any of the previous good lots, except now the bell shaped curve was moved over by .2 grams. The three sigma limits of her distribution were now revised to 9.75 grams and 10.65 grams. They are still within the specification limits so we're OK there. We may have a problem with material costs though because these parts are heavier than they need be.

Statistical Process Control

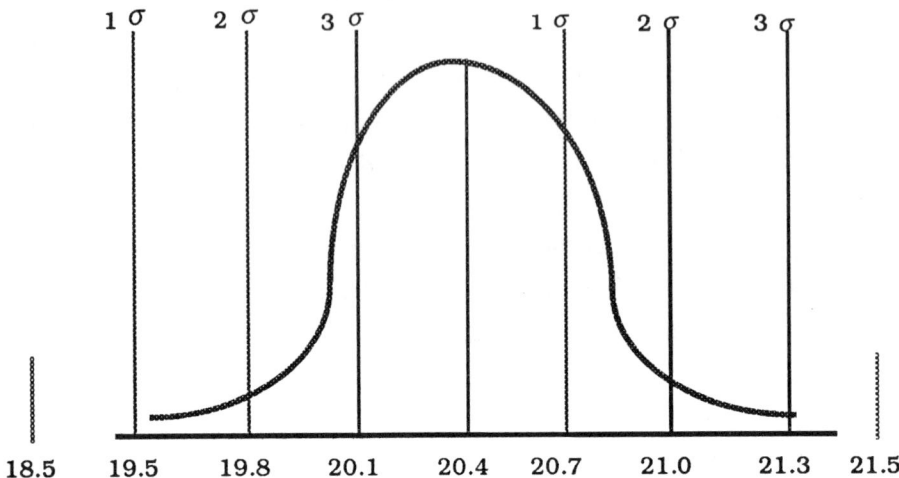

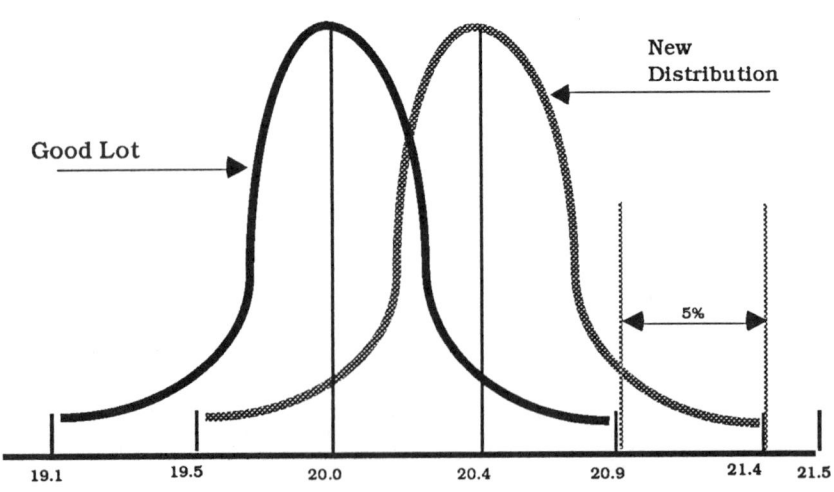

We've already seen that a good lot can vary between 9.55 grams and 10.45 grams. Five percent of the lids off the misadjusted machine were over the limit of 10.45 grams.

This was determined by using the information on the areas under the normal curve as shown in Table I in the appendix.

The difference our new average lid size and the largest to be expected from a good lot is:

average:	new lot	10.2
largest:	good lot	10.45
	difference =	.25 grams

sigma = .15 grams

To convert this .25 grams to standard deviations:

$$\frac{.25}{.15} = 1.67 \text{ standard deviations.}$$

Table I shows the proportion of the process output beyond a single specification limit that is z standard deviation units away from the process average.

Looking up 1.67 standard deviations in the table, we find that 4.75% (rounded to 5%) of the new distribution lies beyond the 20.45 gram point, hence the 5% difference.

If we were to pick up single pieces from the machine with the new adjustment, there are only five chances in one hundred or one chance in twenty that we would get one of the pieces larger than 10.45 grams.

Even if we do find one of these large lids, the way people are sometimes, it could be claimed that it was just one of those freaks that happen sometimes.

Using Control Charts

We are able to prove our point by plotting the output on a **control chart.**

The concepts that we have covered so far are those that are used to construct control charts.

If you recall the earlier discussion where we said the chances of finding a coffee mug with an inside diameter greater than 2.87 inches were one in 740, we were just betting we would not exceed the three sigma limit.

Now let's go back to the coffee mug example and look at the average of the next two mugs coming in at random. It would be a safe assumption that the average diameter of the two will be nearer the grand average of 2.832 inches than to the widest diameter of 2.87 inches.

For the same odds of 740 to 1, we would have to use the narrower three sigma limits. If we were to bet on the average of the next four mugs we would have to use narrower limits still.

Limits for the average of two coffee mugs would be about two-thirds of the limits for individuals. For the average of four mugs the limits would be one half the limits for individuals, and for averages of ten mugs, the limits would be about one third of the limits for individuals.

We got these figures because sample averages vary in the same pattern about the same center as do individual measurements.

The standard deviation of the sample averages is the sigma of the individuals divided by the square root of the sample size.

In the case of the coffee mugs, the sigma of the individual dimensions is 0.01141". For each sample size we divide 0.01141" by the square root of the sample size.

3σ limits

Sample Size n	$\sqrt{n}$	$\dfrac{.01141}{\sqrt{n}}$	$3(\dfrac{.01141}{\sqrt{n}})$	Narrowest $(2.832 - 3\sigma)$	Widest $(2.832 + 3\sigma)$
2	1.414	.0080	.0240	2.808	2.856
4	2.000	.0057	.0171	2.815	2.849
5	2.236	.0051	.0153	2.817	2.847
10	3.162	.0036	.0108	2.821	2.843

Now we can apply this principle to the lids coming off our molding machine.

We take samples of five lids from the machine every twenty minutes and weigh them carefully on a very sensitive scale. We know that the standard deviation of this measurement is .15 grams. Divide this by the square root of five (2.236) and we get a standard deviation of .067 grams for the averages of five lids. Three standard deviations would be 0.202 grams.

If this machine is set properly, for an average of ten grams, averages of five should not vary more than 0.2 grams above and below this center or between 9.8 grams and 10.2 grams.

As long as our samples averages vary between these limits we can be reasonably sure that the actual average of the machine is close to the specified average of ten grams. The odds are 740 to 1 that no sample average will be higher than 10.2 grams.

If the machine setting is 10.2 grams, averages of samples of five will vary .2 grams either side of this higher center. There is now a fifty-fifty chance that any sample average will be above 10.2 grams.

With these odds we're practically certain to get a high average in the first two or three samples.

The control chart is all of the above described in picture form. There are six types of control charts we will be looking at. They are P, C, U, NP, $\overline{X}$ and r, and $\overline{X}$ and s. We will take a good look at each of these charts, but first let's continue with this $\overline{X}$ example.

The center line indicates that the lids should average ten grams. The dotted lines labeled upper and lower control limit say that if the specification is met, the averages of the samples of five should not be less than 9.8 grams or more than 10.2 grams.

From three in the afternoon until seven o'clock, the sample averages stayed between these limits in a pattern we would normally expect.

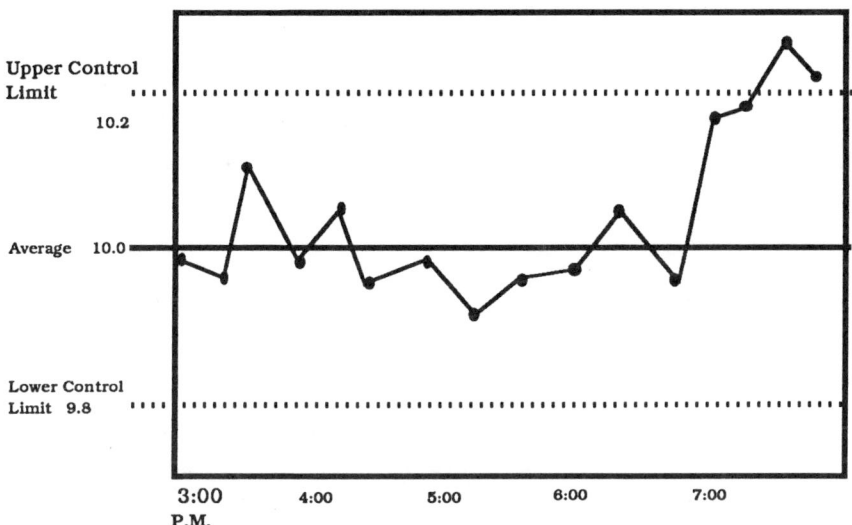

At seven o'clock the pressure transducer which measures cavity pressure blew and it had to be replaced. The operator had a lot on her mind at the time and was in a hurry so she forgot to check the setting carefully. The new setting was actually 10.2 grams.

At seven o'clock, right after the transducer replacement, we measured five lids from the machine. The average was on the high side but it was within the upper control limit so we plotted it on the chart and let it go.

At seven twenty we measured another sample. It was also within the upper control limit on the high side and we know the odds of two samples being so close together near a control limit are very slim. That being the case, we measured another sample right away and this one was beyond the upper control limit.

Just to be sure, we measured one more sample, and it too was beyond the upper control limit.

103

Statistical Process Control

With this evidence on the chart, the operator rechecked her setting, shut down the machine, and re-set the pressure transducer.

After start up, we took some more samples to verify the set up. Everything was all right so we went back to our twenty minute schedule of sampling. The control chart shows us we're OK.

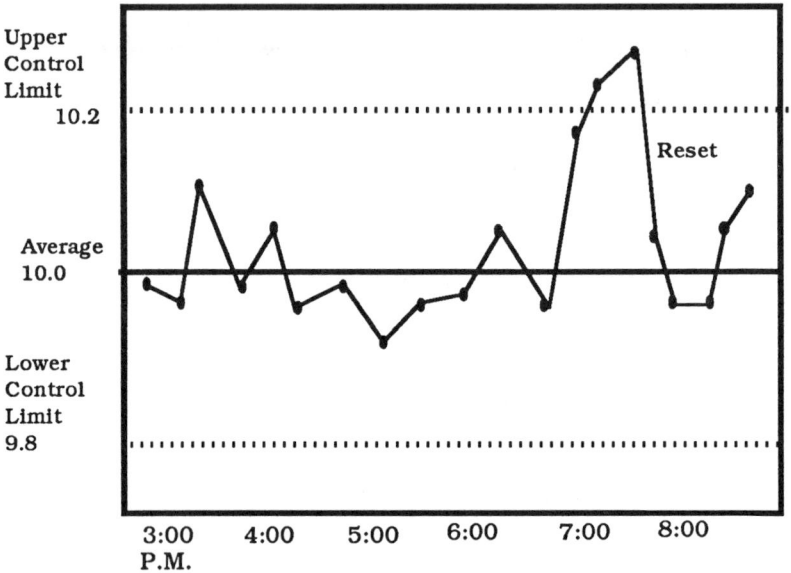

With this background, we're now ready to proceed along with the concept of a process control system.

The Process Control System

Rules are mostly made to be broken
and are too often for the lazy to hide behind

Douglas Macarthur

The primary focus of this section will be to learn what is meant by a process, a process control system, and how to use statistical thinking and methods to improve processes.

The Process

The process begins with a group of people who really want to do a good job. It is often observed that the philosophy that most people want to do a good job is troublesome to many. This can be a very serious problem because it is one of the cornerstones to real process improvement. Without really embracing this philosophy at a deep level, trying to implement the rest of what will be covered can often be futile.

The management of a group puts in place a system composed of equipment, materials, methods, people, and the environment they work in. If the system is not functioning properly, it is the responsibility of management to take action to improve the system.

In the long run, it is more economical to do things right the first time than to fix them later of sort out the good from the bad.

Process Improvement

There are a number of available actions that can be taken to improve quality and productivity. Among these are a more intelligent design of product for manufacturability and use, improvements in the manufacturing and service processes, and responding to the customer's needs.

These methods are not a quick fix. It takes time to implement what we will be covering and once implemented, statistical methods must be used forever to achieve constant improvement.

Eighty-five percent of the problems in manufacturing as well as non manufacturing operations can be traced to a failure on the part of management.

Now let's go on and take a look at what is meant by a **process control system.**

The total performance of a process is measured by the quality of its output and its productive efficiency. These depend on the way it has been designed, built, and the way it is operated. Everything else about the process is useful only if it contributes to the improved performance of the process.

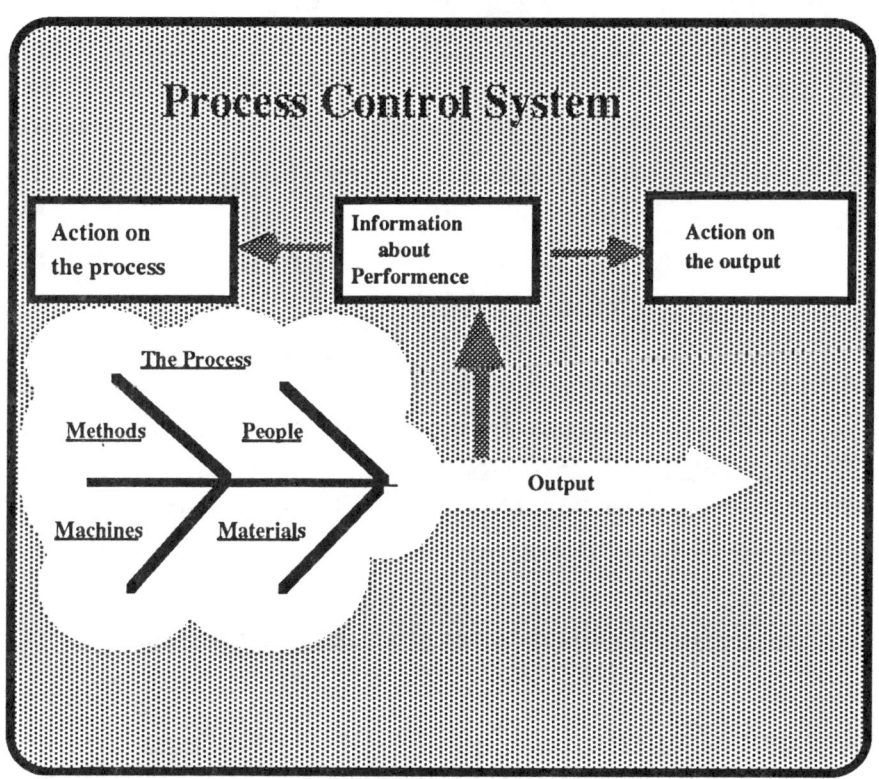

We get information about performance from examining the output of the entire process such as the products it produces or by examining intermediate inputs such as times, temperatures, pressures, etc. If this information is gathered and interpreted correctly, it can show whether action is necessary.

Action on the process is *future oriented* as it is taken when necessary to prevent the output of a bad product. It generally consists of finding and reducing sources of variation.

Action on the output is *past oriented* and consists of things like sorting, redoing the work, managing claims, etc., These actions must continue until actions on the process have been taken and verified or the specifications we are working to have been changed.

The variation that we talked about earlier can affect the process output. As we gather the information about performance, that information, if measured properly begins to form that old familiar pattern called the normal curve.

We could be measuring product size, temperatures, on time delivery, flaws in a bolt of fabric, or the number of parts coming off an operation over time. If our process is being subjected to only the variation from the normal operation of the system, the distribution of these measurements will be normal. If this is the case, we say only common causes of variation are present.

Special and Common Causes of Variation

If, as in the case of the molding machine, there are abnormal or intermittent influences which lead to erratic or unpredictable behavior, we say there are special causes of variation present in addition to the common causes we would expect to find.

Distributions can differ in:

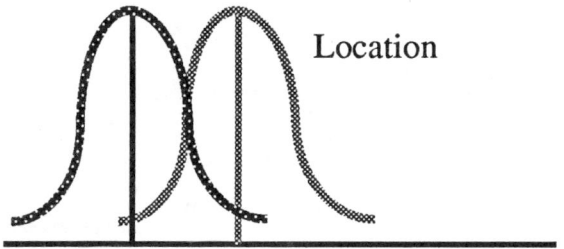

Location

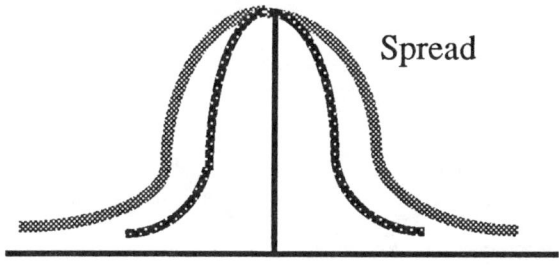

Spread

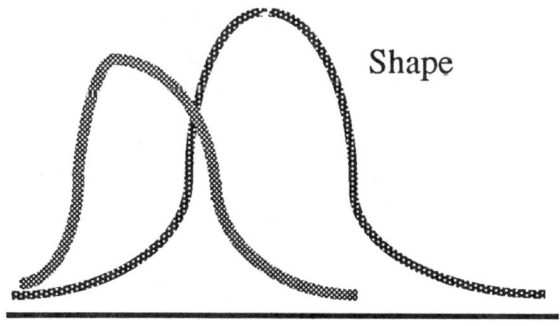

Shape

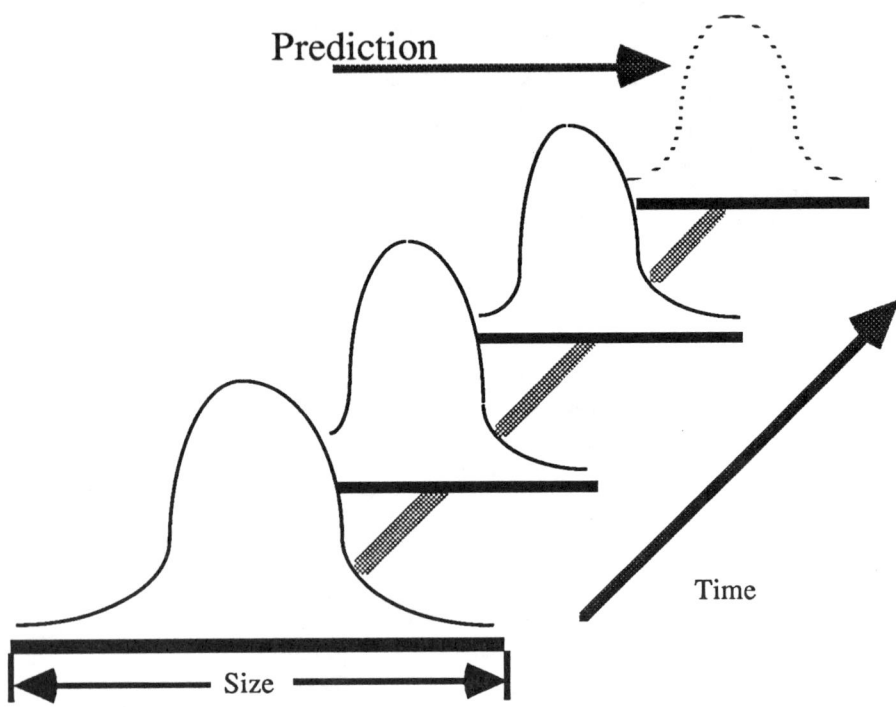

If only common causes of variation are present, the output of a process is stable over time and is predictable.

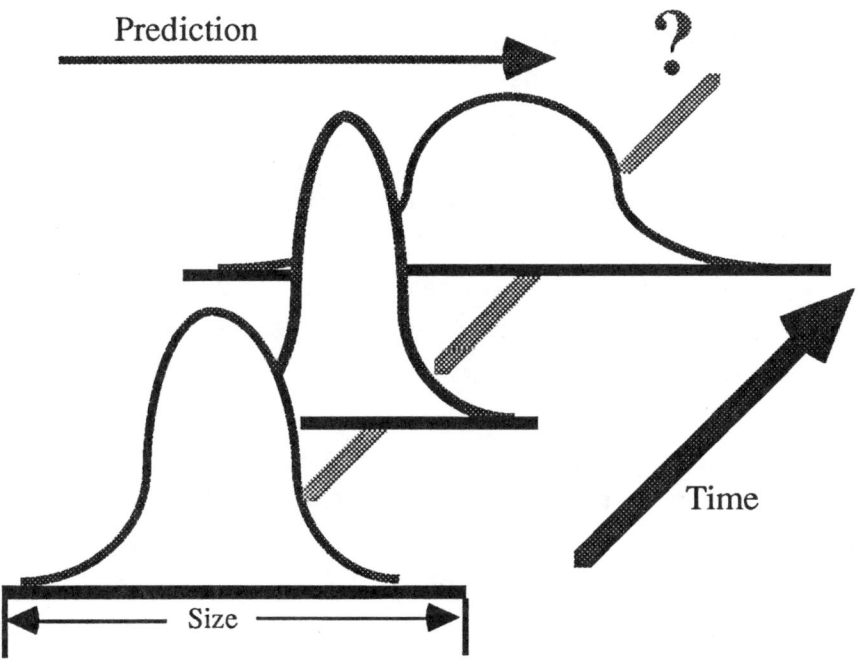

If special causes of variation are present, the process output is not stable over time and is not predictable.

Any process contains many sources of variability. Whether it be large or small, it is always present.

Process Control System

For example, the time to enter an order could vary according to:

* the people performing the various steps
* the reliability of any office equipment they were using
* the accuracy and legibility of the customer's order
* procedures followed
* the volume of other work in the office

To manage and improve the process, the variation must be traced back to its sources. From there it is necessary to distinguish between common and special causes.

Common Causes   The many sources of variation within a process that is in statistical control. Individual values are different but form a distribution pattern characterized by a typical value (average), spread, and shape.

Special Causes   Any factors causing variation that cannot be explained by a single distribution of the process outputs as would be the case in statistical control.

All special causes of variation must be identified and corrected or they will continue to affect the process in unpredictable ways.

Special causes tend to be local in nature and as such local actions are usually required to eliminate them. These actions can usually be taken by people close to the process and it can be said that they can deal with about 15% of the process that is not management's responsibility.

112

A process like the molding machine was in statistical control as long as the sample averages plotted within the upper and lower control limits of the control chart. (There are other aspects of chart interpretation that determine statistical control that will be covered in the upcoming section on control charts.)

It is important to realize that the state of statistical control is not a natural state for a manufacturing process. It is instead an achievement, arrived at by the elimination, one by one, by determined effort, of special causes of variation.

Using Control Charts

Now we will begin to explore different types of control charts and how they can be used. Although these charts can be quite different from one another, there is a common four step process that is used with each.

Four step process for chart utilization

1. Gather data and plot it on the most appropriate type of chart
2. Calculate control limits using simple formulas and indicate them on the chart.
3. Identify special causes of variation and take local actions to correct
4. Quantify common causes of variation and then take action on the system.

Process Control System

The P Chart

Now we're back in our plant again only this time we are measuring the results of a screen printing operation. Each day we audit 1000 items and record the number that are not printed acceptably for whatever reason. The inspection results for twenty days are:

Day	Number of Nonconforming	Fraction Nonconforming
1	28	.028
2	36	.036
3	42	.042
4	35	.035
5	40	.040
6	41	.041
7	33	.033
8	37	.037
9	44	.044
10	40	.040
11	39	.039
12	45	.045
13	42	.042
14	29	.029
15	28	.028
16	25	.025
17	60	.060
18	76	.076
19	31	.031
20	37	.037

We are next going to plot this data on a chart for fraction nonconforming. This is commonly called a **P chart** for percent defective. The fraction nonconforming will be plotted down the side of the chart and the days or sample number are indicated along the bottom.

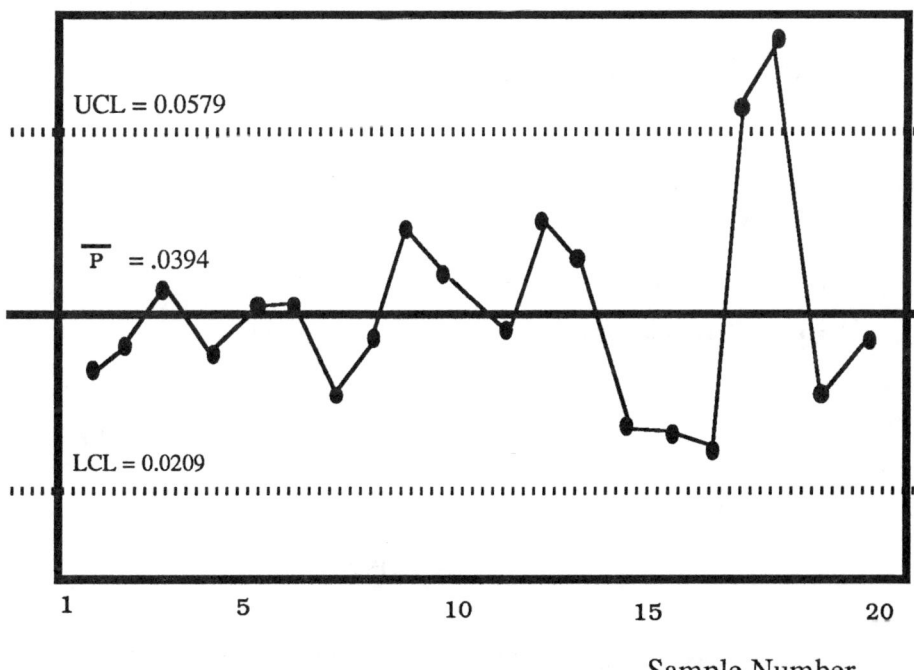

Sample Number

Process Control System

On this type of chart we use the following to calculate the center line and approximate three sigma control limits.

Center Line = $\overline{P}$ =

$$\frac{\text{number of nonconforming units}}{\text{number of units inspected}} = \frac{788}{20000} = 0.394$$

Lower Control Limit: $\quad \text{LCL}_p = \overline{P} - 3\sqrt{\dfrac{\overline{P}(1-\overline{P})}{n}}$

$$3\sqrt{\frac{(.0394)(1-.0394)}{1000}}$$

$$= 0.0209$$

Upper Control Limit: $\quad \text{UCL}_p = \overline{P} + 3\sqrt{\dfrac{\overline{P}(1-\overline{P})}{n}}$

$$= .0394 + 3\sqrt{\frac{(.0394)(1-.0394)}{1000}}$$

$$= 0.0579$$

In this case, it appears that points number 17 and 18 require some further investigation as to what local circumstances may have caused these points to be out of control.

As for the new formula to calculate control limits, the $\overline{X}$ chart which we first looked at is the only instance in the application of the control chart model where the distribution of the individual variables can be shown to tend toward a normal distribution. In the other cases it is sufficient to say that the chance occurrance of a point falling outside 3 sigma limits is very unlikely.

This is not to say that it is impossible to relate probability values with points outside control limits but just that these calculations would be very time consuming especially with P charts where sample sizes vary, and they would contribute little to our decision making.

As a general rule you can say they are of the same order of magnitude as the probability of a point falling outside 3 sigma limits drawing from a normal lot.

In any case, we're not finished evaluating this chart. We are up to the third step where we evaluate special causes of variation. Since we have evidence that something special occurred at points 17 and 18, the data with those points should be removed when calculating the center line and control limits.

This will prevent the data from these two points from influencing what we can normally expect to find. When we do this and recalculate for the remaining 18 samples we find:

Center line: .0362
Upper Control Limit: .0539
Lower Control Limit: .0185

Even with this done, we're still not complete in evaluating all the aspects of what a chart can tell us.

Patterns of Runs

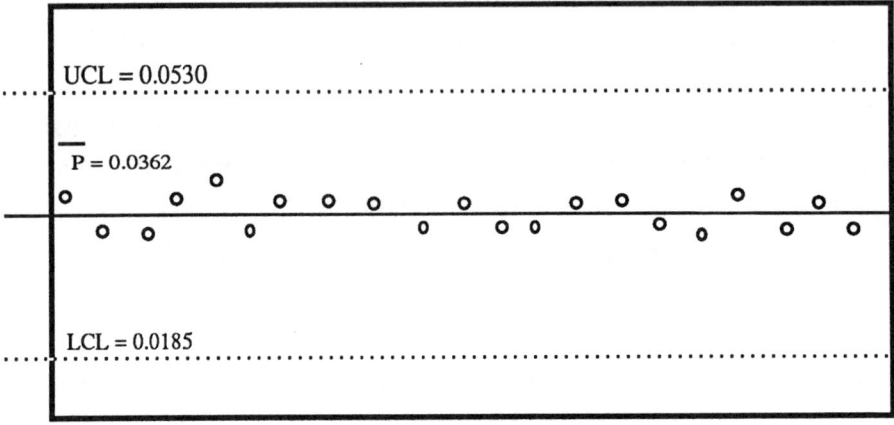

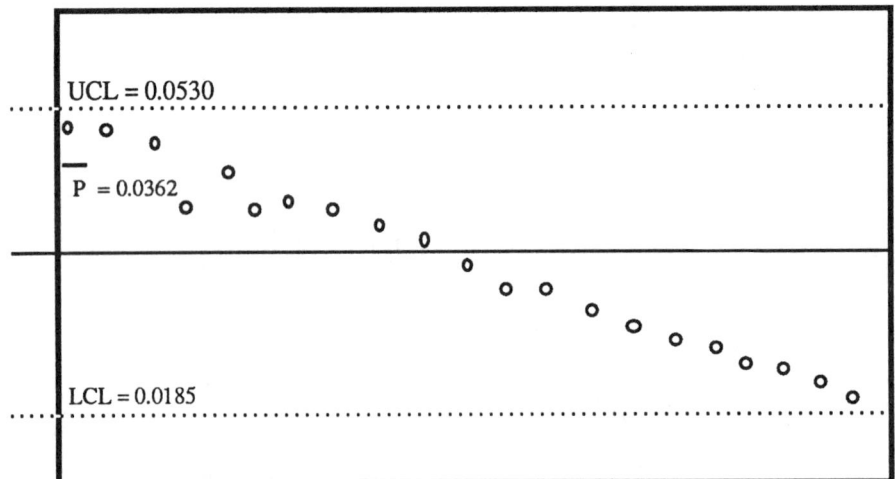

In each of these cases, the pattern of the plotted points shows that things may not be normal even though all points are within the control limits.

Runs Tests Table

Count the number of points above the center line, and also count the number of points below the centerline. Let s = the smaller of these two counts, and l = the larger of these two counts.

Critical Values For Too Few Runs

The probability of finding an equal or smaller number of runs than the number listed is no larger than .05 when there are only random influences present.

s l	5	6	7	8	9	10	11	12	13	14	15	16	17	18	19	20
5	3															
6	3	3														
7	3	4	4													
8	3	4	4	5												
9	4	4	5	5	6											
10	4	5	5	6	6	6										
11	4	5	5	6	6	7	7									
12	4	5	6	6	7	7	8	8								
13	4	5	6	6	7	7	8	8	9							
14	5	5	6	7	7	8	8	9	9	10						
15	5	6	6	7	8	8	9	9	10	10	11					
16	5	6	6	7	8	8	9	10	10	11	11	11				
17	5	6	7	7	8	9	9	10	10	11	11	12	12			
18	5	6	7	8	8	9	10	10	11	11	12	12	13	13		
19	5	6	7	8	8	9	10	10	11	12	12	13	13	14	14	
20	5	6	7	8	9	9	10	11	11	12	12	13	13	14	14	15

Another test we must perform to determine if the patterns are normal is to count the number of runs. In our first P chart we find l=10, and s=8. Our critical value is 6.

A run is the number of times a line connecting the points crosses the center line (or each cluster of points on either side of the center line)

Since we have 10 runs, we have met this criteria and still appear normal. Examples number 2 and 3 would not have passed and will have to be investigated further.

Lastly, we have to test for the length of the longest run. Again for this first P chart: l=10, and s=8, so our critical value is 7. Since our longest run is 6 (point 8 thru 13) we pass this test also.

Again, the runs in examples 2 and 3 are too long which would indicate another reason for further investigation.

Critical Values For Length Of Longest Run

l \ s	5	5	7	8	9	10	11	12	13	14	15	16	17	18	19	20
5	5															
6	6	6														
7	6	6	6													
8	7	7	7	7												
9	8	7	7	7	7											
10	8	8	7	7	7	7										
11	9	8	8	8	7	7	7									
12	10	9	9	8	8	8	8	8								
13	10	10	9	9	8	8	8	8	8							
14	11	10	10	9	9	8	8	8	8	8						
15	11	11	10	10	9	9	9	8	8	8	8					
16	12	11	11	10	10	9	9	9	8	8	8	8				
17	13	12	11	11	10	10	9	9	9	9	8	8	8			
18	13	12	12	11	11	10	10	9	9	9	9	9	9	9		
19	14	13	12	12	11	11	10	10	9	9	9	9	9	9	9	
20	15	14	13	12	11	11	10	10	10	9	9	9	9	9	9	9

The NP Chart

Back in our cap department, we are cutting and sewing up domestic made caps. Each day we set aside 500 caps to be 100% inspected. We have recorded the number of bad caps in each lot of 500 and the results of the first 20 days are given as follows.

Day (Sample Number)	Number of Nonconforming Caps
1	14
2	15
3	14
4	12
5	17
6	15
7	16
8	13
9	13
10	16
11	18
12	15
13	14
14	18
15	17
16	13
17	15
18	16
19	17
20	12

Number of Nonconforming Caps in Lots of 500

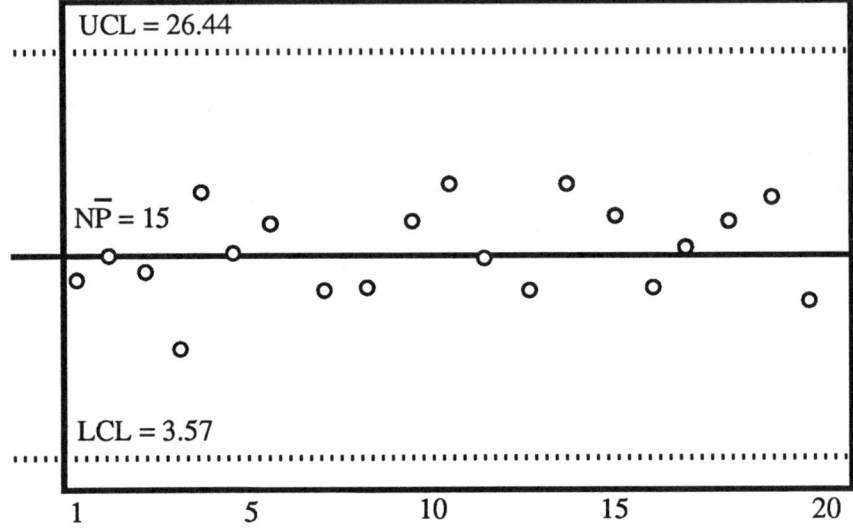

Sample Number

For the NP chart:

Center Line = $N\overline{P}$

$$\overline{P} = \frac{\text{number of nonconforming units}}{\text{total number of units}}$$

$$N\overline{P} = (500)\frac{(300)}{(10,000)} = (500)(0.03) = 15$$

Lower Control Limit:

$$LCL_{np} = N\overline{P} - 3\sqrt{N\overline{P}(1-\overline{P})}$$

$$LCL = 15 - 3\sqrt{(500)(0.03)(1-0.03)} = 3.5565$$

122

Upper Control Limit:

$$UCL_{NP} = N\overline{P} + 3\sqrt{N\overline{P}(1-\overline{P})}$$
$$UCL = 15 + 3\sqrt{(500)(0.03)(1-0.03)} = 26.4435$$

A first glance at the data plotted on an NP control chart indicates only a random pattern to the data, all of which falls within the control limits.

Remember, we have to do all the runs tests to complete our check for only common causes of variation.

On this particular chart, a few of the points lie right on the centerline. A rule of thumb for when that occurs is place these points on either side of the center line that helps you the most in proving a random (normal) pattern.

First; checking for the number of runs;

l = 11; s = 9; therefore the critical value is 6.

If the number of runs on the chart is six or larger then we conclude there is no evidence of non random influences (special causes). For this chart, we call the points on the centerline "below" to help us. We find 10 runs and conclude there are only random influences (common causes) present.

Lastly: checking for the length of the longest run.

l = 11; s = 9; therefore the critical value is 7

Our longest run is four which is smaller than the critical value so we conclude there is no evidence of non random influences.

Since we have only common causes of variation, we have a stable process that will not improve until management takes action on the system.

Process Control System

Control Limits for Varying Sample Sizes

In one part of our mug operation, water slide decals are hand applied to coffee mugs. For the last twenty days we have studied this process and for each day we recorded the number of misapplied decals. The number of mugs decorated varied from day to day. Here are the results of this study.

Day	Number of Mugs	Number Misapplied	Fraction Misapplied
1	750	54	.072
2	750	39	.052
3	250	28	.112
4	250	17	.068
5	250	13	.052
6	1000	78	.078
7	1000	65	.065
8	750	72	.096
9	500	22	.044
10	500	31	.062
11	1000	74	.074
12	1000	56	.056
13	250	28	.112
14	1000	94	.094
15	1000	80	.080
16	500	48	.096
17	250	22	.088
18	750	69	.092
19	750	60	.080
20	250	27	.108

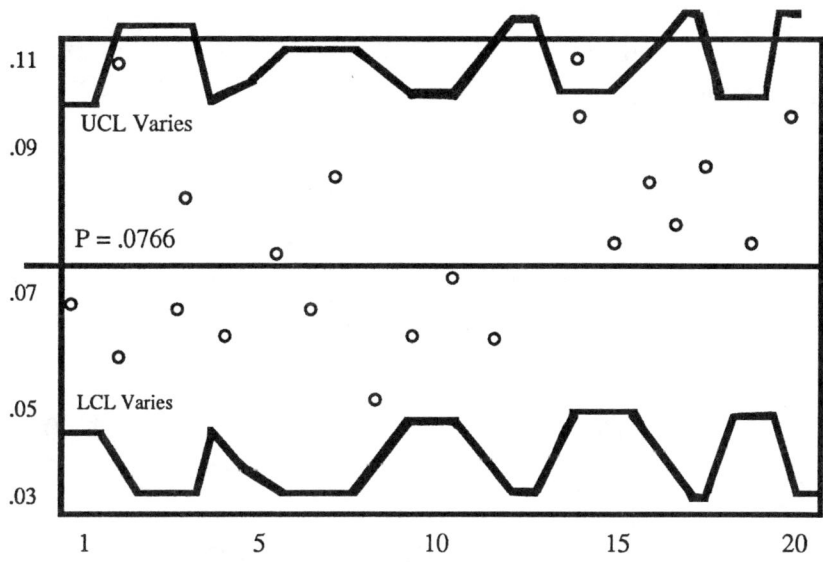

We have a new twist here in that the number of mugs we looked at was different every day. This won't affect the way we calculate the average but it will mean that the control limits must be recalculated each time the sample size changes because according to the formula, they will vary with the size of the sample.

Reviewing the P chart formulas;

$$\text{Center Line} = \overline{P} = \frac{\text{number of nonconforming units}}{\text{total number of units}}$$

$$\text{Lower Control Limit} = \overline{P} - 3\sqrt{\frac{\overline{P}(1-\overline{P})}{n}}$$

$$\text{Upper Control Limit} = \overline{P} + 3\sqrt{\frac{\overline{P}(1-\overline{P})}{n}}$$

125

Process Control System

Where we have several sample sizes but some repetition or a repeat of sample sizes we can set these calculations up in a simple table.

$$\overline{P} = \frac{977}{12750} = .0766$$

n	$\overline{P}$	$\pm 3\sqrt{\dfrac{\overline{P}(1-\overline{P})}{n}}$	UCL	LCL
250	.0766	.050	.126	.026
500	.0766	.0355	.116	.040
750	.0766	.029	.105	.047
1000	.0766	.025	.101	.051

The same principle holds true for *NP* Charts. The center line, lower control limit, and upper control limit all vary with the sample size.

In an operational environment where you make the decision to track output at the end of a shift, day, etc., and you can expect the sample sizes to vary, it will be necessary to calculate control limits for each point on the chart if we are to expect clean information as to whether what we look at is normal.

Now look at what happens in this case where we chart an operation that is running three shifts.

Charting Separate Shifts or Groups

The following data represent visual defects found during periodic audits of a pen printing operation. The data cover the output of a single printing machine working three shifts a day over a two week period.

Twice during each shift, at times varying from day to day, a sample of 200 pens was taken. The pens were inspected on a brightly lit table by a specially trained inspector who recorded the number of defectives found.

Visual Inspection of Screen Printed Writing Instruments

Week 1

1st Shift	Mon	Tue	Wed	Thu	Fri	Sat
Sample1	3	3	5	3	5	2
Sample2	2	0	0	3	1	3
2nd Shft						
Sample1	2	3	5	5	3	9
Sample2	3	6	5	10	6	3
3rd Shft						
Sample1	4	5	3	5	2	5
Sample2	1	3	2	1	5	3

Week 2

1st Shift	Mon	Tue	Wed	Thu	Fri	Sat
Sample1	2	2	4	2	4	0
Sample2	5	5	2	3	2	6
2nd Shft						
Sample1	4	8	5	4	2	11
Sample2	6	7	5	6	3	2
3rd Shft						
Sample1	2	5	5	2	3	6
Sample2	4	4	3	3	3	1

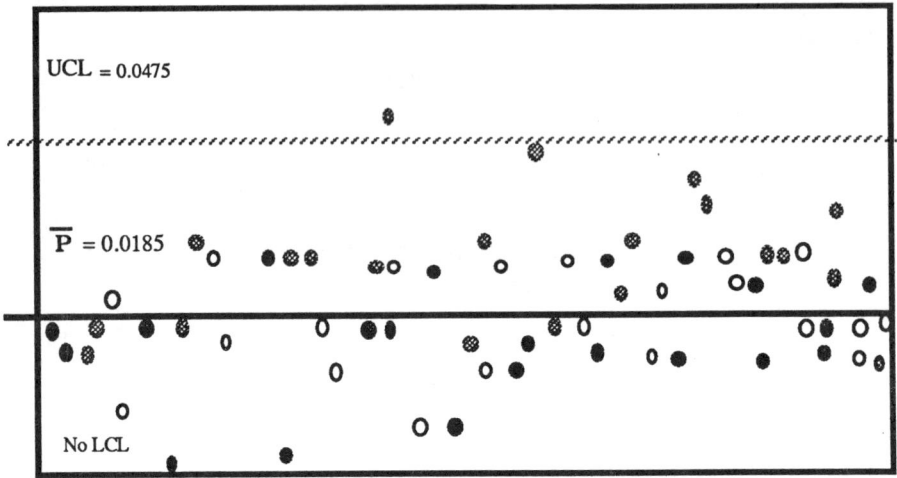

As we plot this data on a control chart, we get an indication that something special has caused two points to go out of control. Further investigation shows that those two points plus the other three points closest to the upper control limit occurred on the second shift.

This leads to the decision to evaluate the data from each shift separptely.

Here are the control charts for each shift.

Visual Inspection of Screen Printed Pens   1St Shift

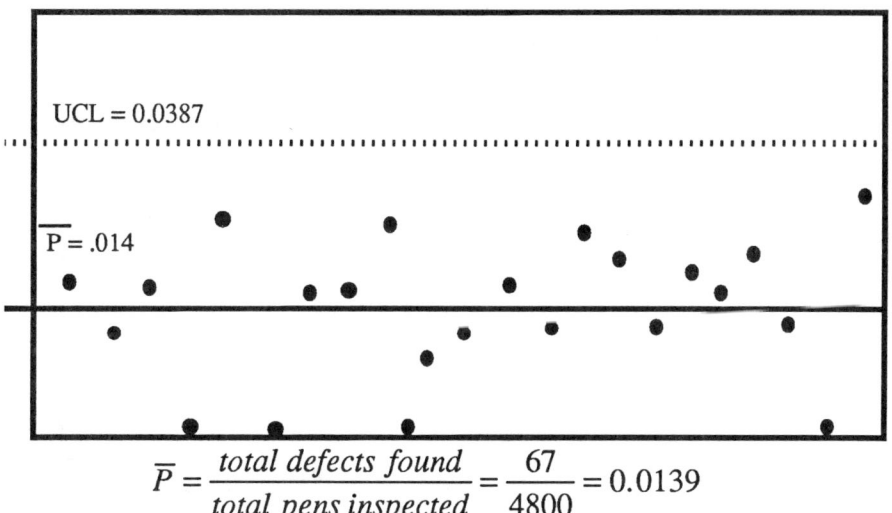

$$\overline{P} = \frac{total\ defects\ found}{total\ pens\ inspected} = \frac{67}{4800} = 0.0139$$

$$UCL = \overline{P} + 3\sqrt{\frac{\overline{P}(1-\overline{P})}{n}} = 0.0139 + 3\sqrt{\frac{(0.0139)(1-0.0139)}{200}}$$

$$= 0.0139 + 0.0248 = 0.0387$$

There is no lower control limit.

Process Control System

A further check will show that this distribution passes both runs tests so we can say that the first shift shows evidence of statistical stability with only common causes of variation present.

Looking at the other two shifts:

Visual Inspection of Screen Printed Pens   **2nd Shift**

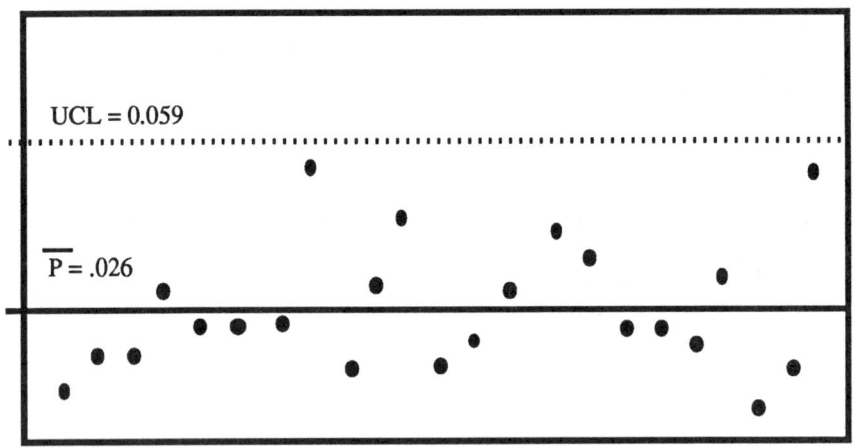

$$\overline{P} = \frac{123}{4800} = 0.0256 \quad UCL = 0.0256 + 3\sqrt{\frac{(0.0256)(1 - 0.0256)}{200}}$$

$$= 0.0256 + 0.0335 = 0.059$$

No Lower Control Limit
This distribution has all points in statistical control and passes both runs tests.

Visual Inspection of Screen Printed Pens   3rd Shift

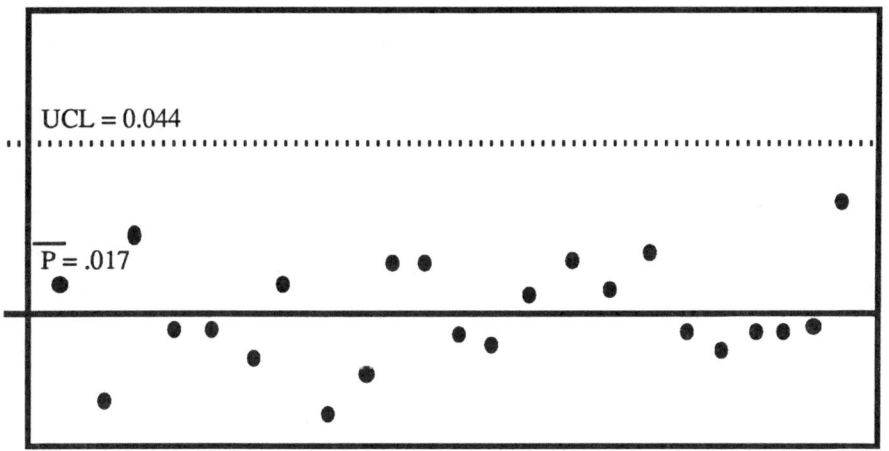

$$\overline{P} = \frac{80}{4800} = 0.0167 \quad UCL = 0.0167 + 3\sqrt{\frac{(0.0167)(1-0.0167)}{200}}$$

$$= 0.0167 + 0.0272 = 0.0439$$

No lower control limit

This distribution also has all points in statistical control and passes both runs tests.

Put all three of these shifts together on the same chart and there is no evidence of statistical control.

Separately the data and charting each shift separately shows that each shift is operating under statistical control within itself. They show only common causes of variation and again it is unlikely that they will change until management takes action on their system.

Differences Among Different Shifts or Groups

There are a couple of points that need to be covered regarding the differences in performance among the shifts.

First, the differences may not be statistically significant. As we learn to evaluate data statistically we begin to understand that although absolute values may be different, it is possible, due to normal variation, that they could come from the same system.

There are tests (which we will get into shortly) that can be used on distributions like these that help us to determine if the differences we are looking at are statistically significant.

Secondly, and this assumes that the differences are significant, evaluating differences in operations in this manner allows us to find where the secret knowledge is in our company. If we like what the people with the secret knowledge are doing, we find out what it is and exploit it. In this case we would try to determine what if any secret knowledge is on the first shift.

Conversely, it may be that we don't like what the people with the secret knowledge are doing and we would want to isolate it and eliminate it. It may be in our case here that the second shift has their own preferred way to set up the machine and that is actually hurting them.

In any case, now that we have each shift plotted separately, our investigations into our pen screen printing operation will be a great deal more enlightened.

The U Chart

In our cutting and sewing operations we have decided to begin measuring the incoming quality from our textile vendors. Over a ten week period we visually inspected the bolts of cloth as they were spread on the cutting table and recorded the data below.

Day	Bolts inspected	Number of imperfections	Nonconformities per unit
1	20	27	1.35
2	20	23	1.15
3	20	30	1.50
4	21	28	1.33
5	22	29	1.32
6	22	31	1.41
7	23	37	1.61
8	33	29	0.88
9	23	36	1.57
10	21	27	1.29

We will construct a **U chart** where;

N = the number of units inspected
C = the number of nonconformities

and $U = \dfrac{C}{N} = $ *nonconformities per unit*

Process Control System

$$\overline{U} = \frac{\text{total number of nonconformities}}{\text{total number of units inspected}}$$

Lower Control Limit; $\quad LCL_U = \overline{U} - 3\dfrac{\sqrt{\overline{U}}}{\sqrt{N}}$

Upper Control Limit; $\quad UCL_U = \overline{U} + 3\dfrac{\sqrt{\overline{U}}}{\sqrt{N}}$

The sample size varies for each day so separate control limits for each point will have to be calculated.

$$\overline{U} = \frac{297}{225} = 1.32 \qquad\qquad 3\sqrt{\overline{U}} = 3\sqrt{1.32} = 3.4467$$

Day	N	$\dfrac{3.4467}{\sqrt{N}}$	LCL	UCL
1	20	.77	.55	2.09
2	30	.77	.63	1.95
3	20	.77	.55	2.09
4	21	.75	.57	2.07
5	22	.73	.59	2.05
6	22	.73	.59	2.05
7	23	.72	.60	2.04
8	33	.60	.72	1.92
9	23	.72	.60	2.04
10	21	.75	.57	2.07

Control Chart for Non conformities per Unit   Bolts of Cloth

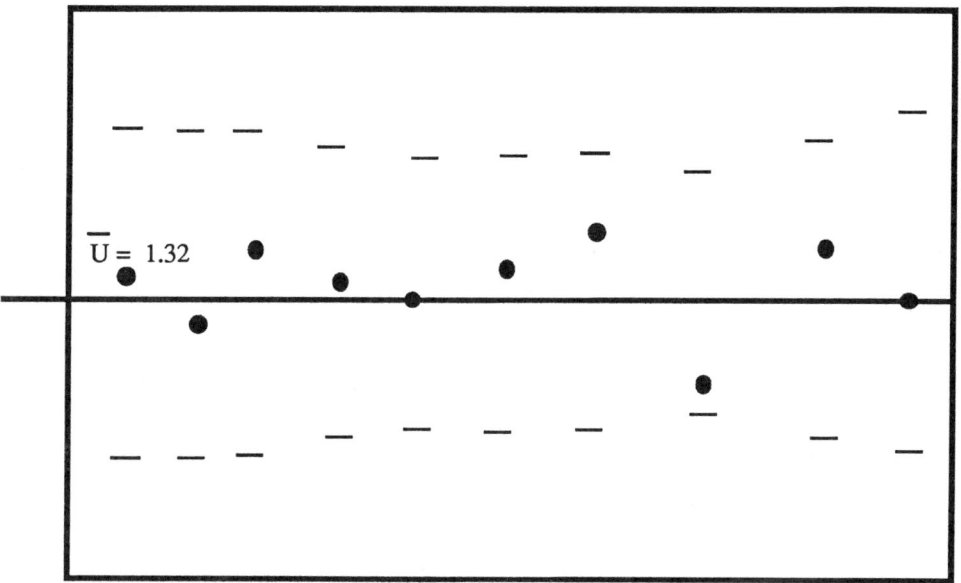

$\overline{U} = 1.32$

All indications are that we have a stable distribution averaging 1.32 defects per bolt which we can expect to remain unchanged until our supplier makes some fundamental process changes.

The C Chart

If we had elected to inspect a constant number of bolts of cloth each day we could have used a C chart that is quite a bit

Process Control System

simpler to use. Here we are inspecting ten bolts per day where ten bolts equal one inspection unit.

Day	Number of Nonconformities	Day	Number of Nonconformities
1	22	11	15
2	29	12	10
3	25	13	33
4	17	14	23
5	20	15	27
6	16	16	17
7	34	17	33
8	11	18	19
9	31	19	22
10	29	20	27

Central LIne: $= \overline{C} = \dfrac{\text{total number of nonconformities}}{\text{total number of inspection units}} = \dfrac{460}{20} = 23$

Contol Limits $= \overline{C} \pm 3\sqrt{\overline{C}} = 23 \pm 3\sqrt{23} = 23 \pm 14.39 =$

UCL = 37.39

LCL = 8.61

Control Chart for Nonconformities per unit   Bolts of Cloth

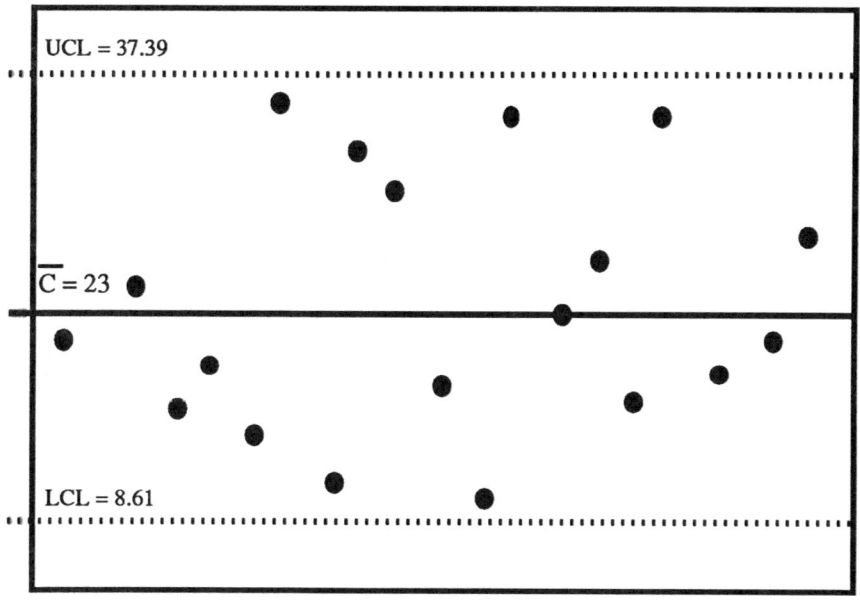

This concludes this section on how to obtain statistical evidence on the output of a process. This is enough information to begin a simple and effective charting program.

In the next section we will cover how to use this information to begin to take corrective action.

Information

Interpretation

Pain makes man think.
Thought makes man wise.
Wisdom makes life endurable.

John Patrick

The Pareto Principle

As we begin further analysis of the sources of variation on control charts we become aware that the causes we turn up may vary in importance.

The same principle that is so easy to grasp when we say that 80% of our sales come from 20% of our customers is becoming apparent here. This phenomena is called the Pareto principle after Vilfredo Pareto, an Italian economist (1848-1923) had studied the distribution of wealth and observed the nonuniformity of its distribution. This principle has also been calleed the 80/20 rule, the law of the vital few, and the law of the significant few.

Some other examples would be in purchasing where a small percentage of the orders amount for most of the dollars spent, or in inventory costs where a few items account for most of the inventory value.

Interpreting the Information

In our work on identifying causes of variation this principle guides our first task and that is **separating the vital few from the trivial many.**

If we don't do a good job here we can find that by assigning equal value to all inputs (or sources of variation) the odds are about 80:20 or four to one that we will spend valuable time and resources working on something trivial that could have little to no effect in improving our processes.

Put another way, it has been said that no intelligent approach to quality improvement is possible without it.

The vital few items we wish to identify are done so through a **"Pareto Analysis"**. Basically, this consists of a listing of the contributions to the problem (in this case finding sources of variation) in the order of their importance.

The following table and visual analysis show how this is done. We'll continue to use the data from the bolts of cloth we inspected for this example.

Nonconformities in Bolts of Cloth

Tears	104
Stains	241
Faded Spots	25
Wrinkles	35
Holes	20
Other	35

Using a declining in order Pareto Analysis, we could construct a table like this:

Defect	Number of Decects	Percentage of total Defects
Stains	241	52.4
Tears	104	22.6
Wrinkles	35	7.6
Faded Spots	25	5.4
Holes	20	4.3
Other	35	7.6

or a graphic presentation like this;

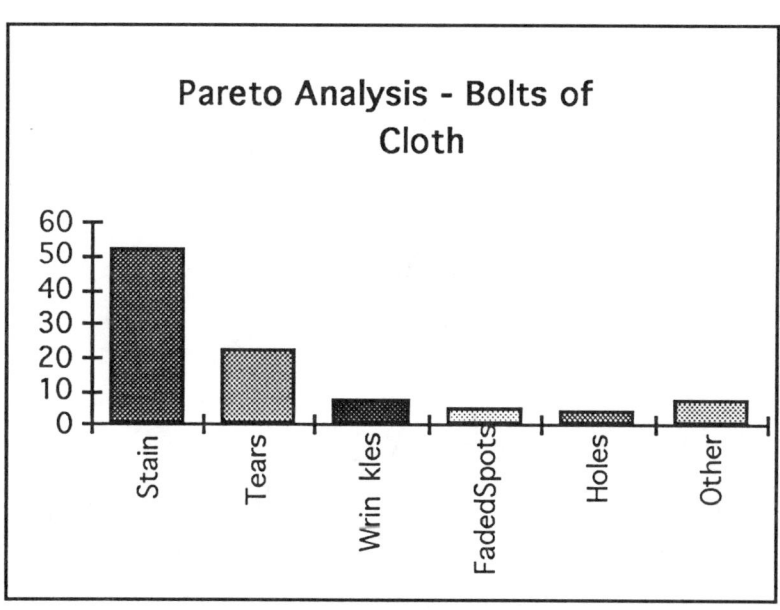

Interpreting the Information

As a result of this analysis, we communicate the stain problem to our supplier and collect another ten days of data inspecting ten bolts a day so ten bolts is our inspection unit.

Day	Number of Nonconformities
1	22
2	18
3	17
4	14
5	18
6	11
7	17
8	12
9	9
10	14
total	152

We continue plotting these points after the first ten points on our C chart.

C Chart Bolts of Cloth

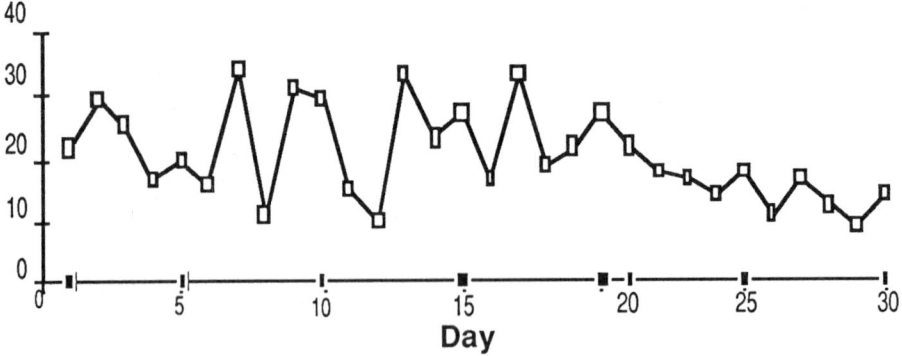

$$\frac{152}{10} = 15.2 = \overline{C} \qquad \overline{C} \pm 3\sqrt{\overline{C}} = 15.2 \pm 11.7$$

The samples inspected after the supplier was shown the problem with the stains showed that the process had shifted. The new data did not pass the runs test using the former center line and control limits.

Statistical Signals

This gave us a **statistical signal** that something had happened to the process to improve it.

In the past, judgements may have been made about points above and below the centerline using words like good, bad, better, or worse. The proper use of statistical techniques makes the use of adjectives like these inappropriate. We are now talking in the language of a **distribution of points** and not the points themselves. The points will naturally vary above and below the centerline as a normal part of the variation in that distribution.

Now the only sound basis for judgement about our process is the distribution of points on our control chart with respect to the *control limits*, *number of runs*, and the *length of the longest run*.

When we receive valid statistical signals like these it now becomes appropriate to conclude that **real change** has occurred to the process.

In our case of the bolts of cloth, the process had shifted as could be seen by the run of ten points below the centerline of the chart. This means we have a new process that will require a recalculation of the centerline and control limits in order to monitor its sources of variation.

In doing so we get;

Center line   15.2

Upper Control Limit   26.9

Lower Control Limit   3.5

Using these criteria to evaluate the new process, we find that we are experiencing only common causes of variation in this new distribution of measurements because it is in statistical control.

Histograms

Constructing and interpreting histograms is another useful method to investigate causes of variation. The histograms we looked at earlier followed the pattern of the normal curve but that is not always the case.

What follows are instructions along with a model of a worksheet used to prepare a histogram.

First determine the range of the data by subtracting the smallest measurement from the largest and record the units of measure. The determine the number of classes needed based on the number of readings taken. (see table)

Calculate the width of each class by dividing the range by the number of classes. Select the first class midpoint which, if possible, should be the largest reading. To determine the upper class limit of the first class, divide the class width by two and add to the class midpoint.

Subsequent class limits can be determined by subtracting the class width from the upper class limit and so forth until the smallest reading is included in the last class

Construct the histogram and plot the frequency of readings that fall within each class. Class limits can be rounded off. Assure that rounded class limits exceed the measurement unit.

Determine if the histogram appears normal. If appropriate, calculate the average, standard deviation, and statistical limits using ± 3 sigma.

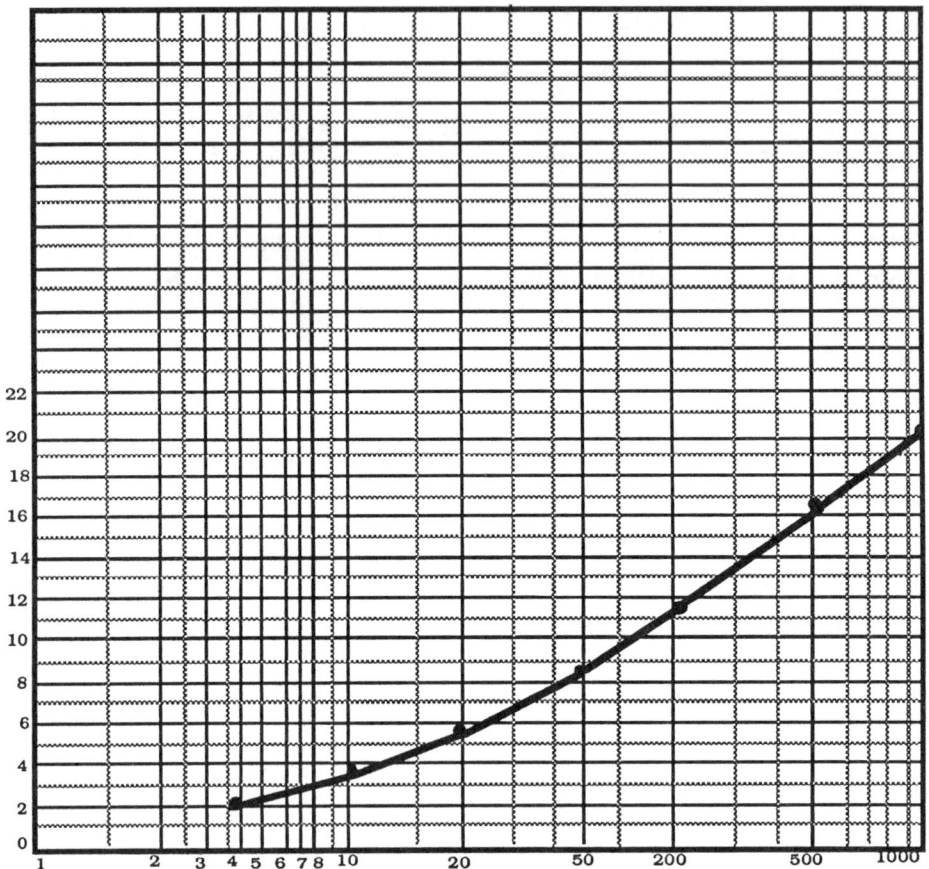

vertical scale = number of classes (k), Horizontal = Number of measurements

We saw a histogram of cup lids in our earlier example. Now lets look at temperature readings for the pre heat zone of a decorating lehr. This is a very critical temperature measurement for if the decorating temperature is not brought up at the correct pace, breakage occurs.

146

Over a two shift decorating operation we have taken fourteen temperature readings a day over five weeks (25 working days) of the pre heat zone.

Here are the results:

Pre heat zone temperarure readings: Oven #1

444	480	480	458	407	492	450	440	479	496	491	480	476	458
480	415	472	476	440	469	458	439	439	475	478	485	471	466
469	439	504	454	493	454	477	481	496	413	501	492	456	481
468	422	429	503	446	493	439	459	444	453	522	441	498	484
461	458	447	459	450	444	461	471	455	441	495	456	450	467
492	476	473	466	437	487	461	460	417	511	467	460	462	453
461	455	481	494	435	493	454	445	418	440	450	466	463	449
484	496	468	503	426	463	460	449	459	482	508	463	457	516
494	423	417	424	460	461	471	477	469	465	473	466	482	421
439	450	475	433	452	442	498	482	474	489	475	445	484	477
440	473	460	469	508	492	493	498	469	468	435	403	490	469
485	454	460	469	501	475	466	444	461	439	478	444	459	482
438	478	468	495	472	483	471	502	450	442	471	456	435	482
451	474	453	445	483	460	460	460	463	511	483	434	478	511
424	398	471	488	459	467	474	432	485	502	469	444	467	447
473	457	447	465	456	494	503	441	477	409	450	485	470	470
454	451	503	459	460	486	450	445	459	479	429	461	446	473
417	493	466	481	477	466	507	476	474	509	446	453	487	448
464	467	446	463	426	474	444	481	501	502	480	464	481	514
465	449	459	507	480	468	493	475	439	475	439	469	462	456
450	465	465	458	447	497	494	521	472	461	483	484	495	499
471	421	462	494	488	455	470	486	460	416	460	500	460	451
497	459	498	518	452	502	475	461	464	521	421	455	456	460
468	495	510	489	421	481	471	439	476	443	435	477	513	472
479	459	457	485	491	476	495	428	422	439	460	448	461	502

Interpreting the Information

The largest reading is 522^0 and the smallest is 398^0 so the range is 124^0.

The units of measure are degrees Fahrenheit and are so recorded on the histogram format.

In referring to Table 1 we find that with 350 readings we should set up fifteen classes and the width of each class will be the range divided by the number of classes.

$$C.W. = Class\ Width\ =\ \frac{R}{k}\ =\frac{124}{15}\ = 8.27$$

$$R = \text{Range}$$

$$k = \text{Number of classes}$$

The first class midpoint is the largest reading.   C.M.P.= 522

The upper class limit:

$$\frac{class\ width}{2} + \textbf{\textit{class midpoint}}$$

$$\frac{8.27}{2} + 522\ =\ 4.135 + 522 = 526.135$$

Subsequent class limits:

$1st\ U.C.L. - C.W.\ =\ 526.135 - 8.27 =$

1) 526.1
2) 517.8
3) 509.5
4) 501.3
5) 493.1
6) 484.8
7) 476.5
8) 468.2
9) 459.9
10) 451.7
11) 443.4
12) 435.2
13) 426.9
14) 418.6
15) 410.4
16) 402.1

Note that it takes sixteen boundaries to define fifteen classes.

The Resulting Histogram

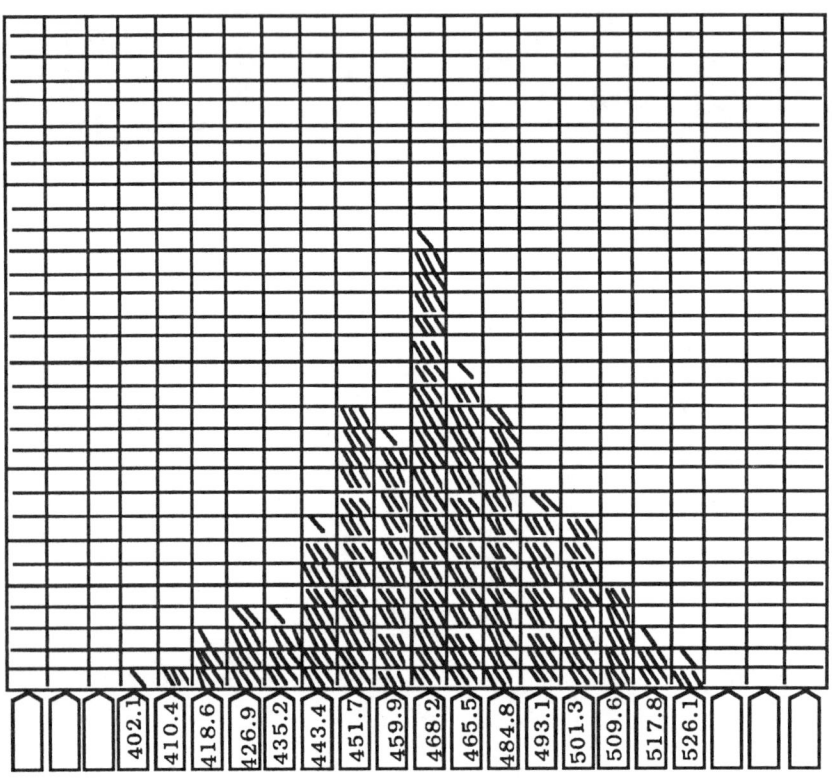

The distribution approximates the normal curve so we can calculate the average, standard deviation, and use ± 3 sigma control limits.

Interpreting Distributions

If the histogram we plot shows a normal distribution we can use that information to extrapolate the future of that process because we are predictable. This holds true whether we are predicting temperature from a distribution of temperature measurements or receipt of good product from a distribution of incoming audit results.

Sometimes the distribution is not normal but you can understand what is happening just by looking at it. Here are a few examples.

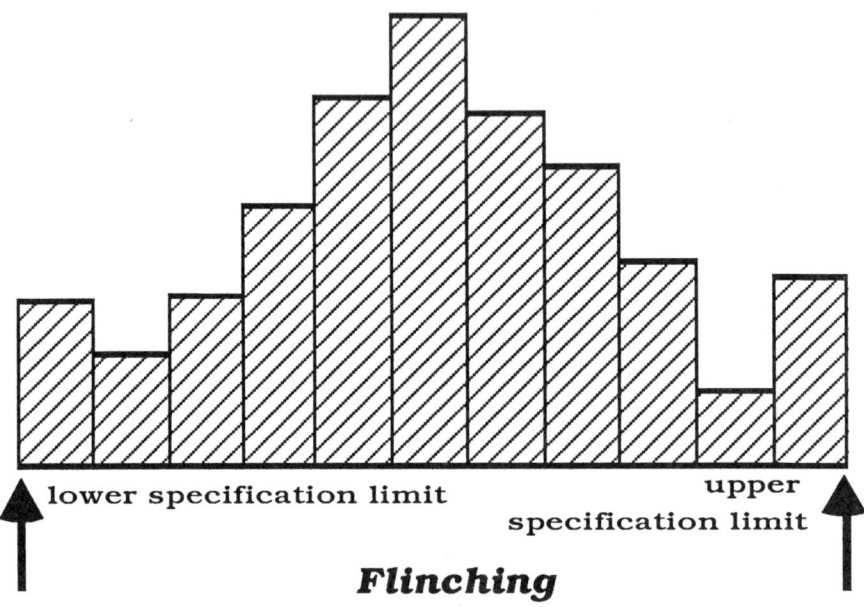

lower specification limit   upper
specification limit

Flinching

    Notice the coincidence that there are no measurements that are beyond the specification limits. If it weren't for the spikes on either end, this could be close to being a normal distribution.

    This phenomena is often called **"flinching"**. It occurs when whoever is doing the measuring is also aware of the specifications. When measurements are just a little over the specification limit they flinch when recording and record an in spec measurement rather than one just a little over.

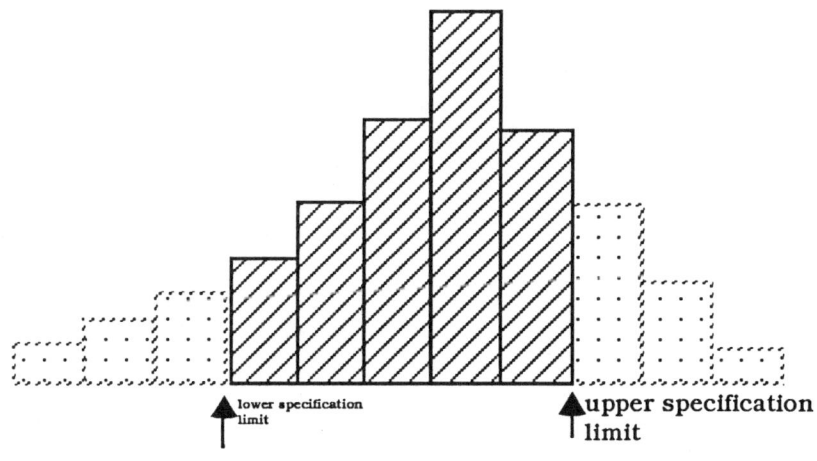

Sorted

This is the typical distribution you would get on parts that have been sorted. The portion of the distribution indicated by the dotted lines is missing because it has been **sorted** out. If as in our coffee mug example we were sampling the inside diameter at receiving and this was the histogram of that audit, we could assume the lot had been sorted previously. The problem with a sorting operation is that some nonconforming product will always find its way through. At least in this case, the process is centered so we're only sorting out a relatively small amount at each extreme.

153

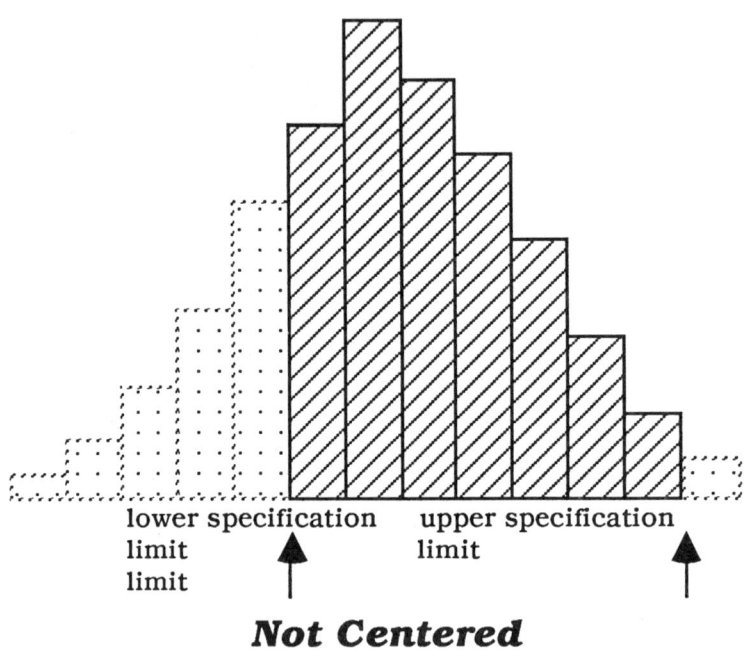

lower specification   upper specification
limit   limit
limit

Not Centered

Here is a sorted distribution with more serious ramnifications. The process is not centered with respect to the specification limits so in the sorting process, even much more of the distribution has to be sorted out.

This not only adds cost to the overall process, it also increases the likelihood of items getting into the system that don't meet the specifications.

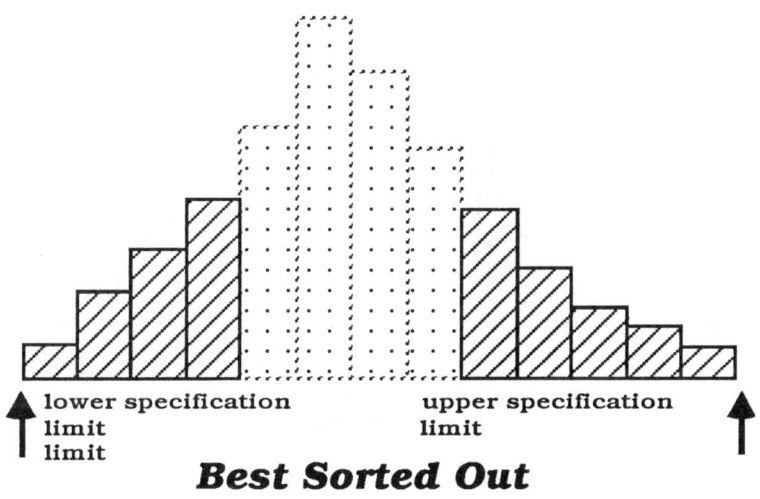

lower specification
limit
limit

upper specification
limit

Best Sorted Out

Here's a distribution pattern you sometimes see when someone else gets the good stuff. Again, using our coffee mug example, if we were to audit the sizes of our incoming mugs and arrived at a distribution like this as the result of that audit, we

Interpreting the Information

would want to know what happened to the mugs that should have been in the middle. Since reduced size variation improves decorating ability, we would want to know where the good mugs went.

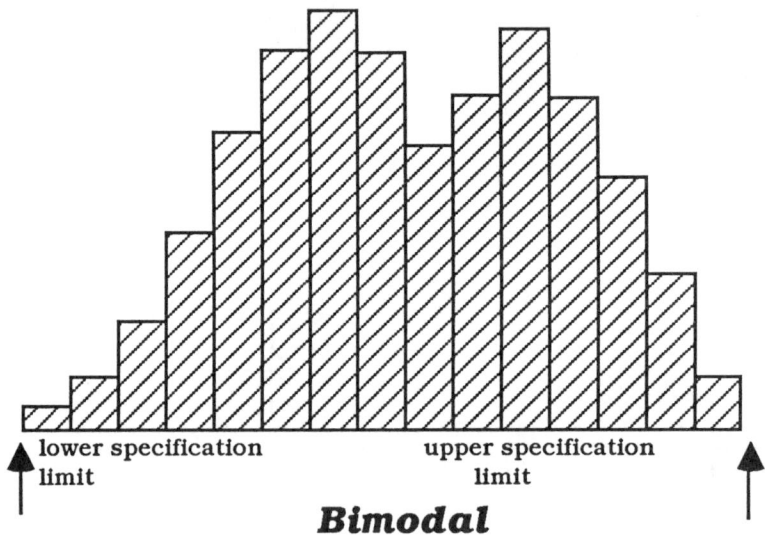

lower specification limit

upper specification limit

Bimodal

This is called a **bimodal distribution** and occurs frequently when two different processes are used to produce the same part. They could come from different machines, departments, plants, or even countries.

Since the driving force behind process improvement is the reduction of variation, you can see why many companies are going to single sources for their raw materials to reduce this type of variability.

Evaluating The Process

*If we could first know where we are,
and whither we are tending,
we could then better judge what to do,
and how to do it.*

Abraham Lincoln

The Central Limit Theorem

From the standpoint of process control, the central limit theorem is one of the most powerful statistical tools there is.

Simply stated, the theorem says:

The distribution of individual readings taken from a process in statistical control may have any conceivable shape.

The distribution of $\overline{X}$ values of samples drawn from that process will be normal provided the sample size is large enough.

Thus we can use the standard normal distribution table we used earlier to evaluate probabilities related to the distribution of sample averages.

This statistic forms the basis of the $\overline{X}$ chart. The sample size does not have to be very large before the normal distribution can be used.

Evaluating the Process

The following diagrams illustrate what typically happens with sample sizes of 2, 5, and 30.

As you can see, once you reach a sample size of five, the distribution of $\overline{X}$ values is normal.

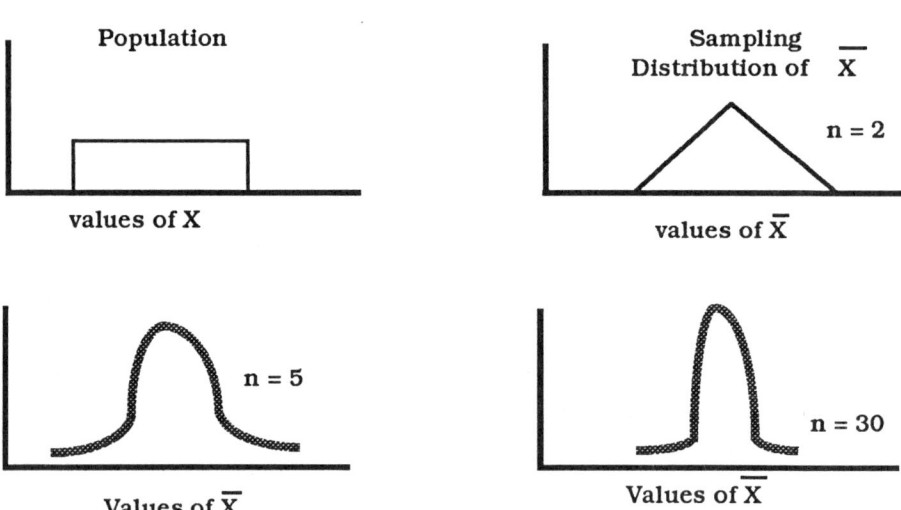

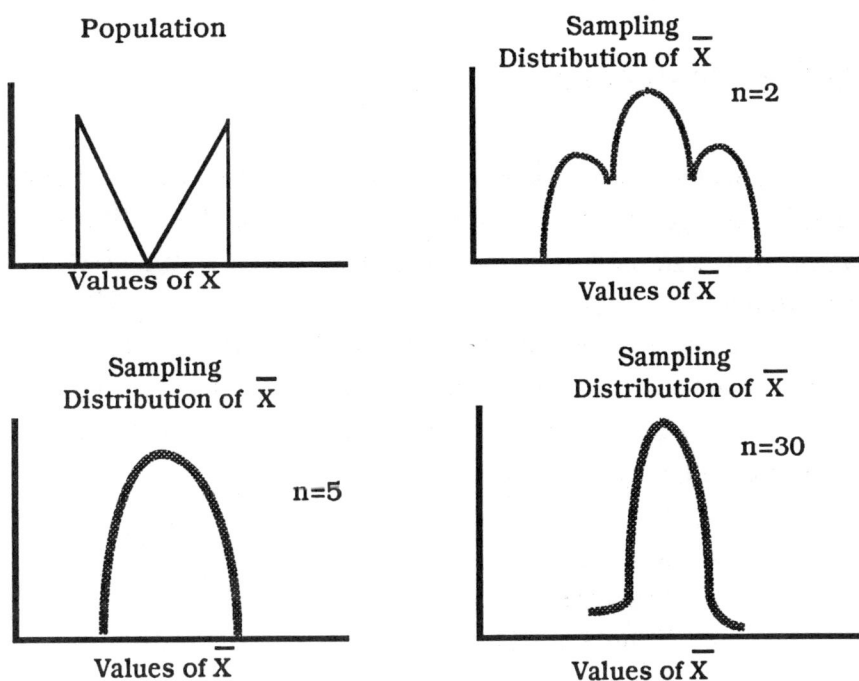

If the distribution of sample averages from any population remains normal then it can be said that there is no statistically significant difference in the distribution of values in the original population. This occurs even when the shape of the original population is other than a normal distribution.

In a round about way we can revert to the average and three sigma limits because the central limit theorem says the distribution of sample averages can meet this criteria.

159

Charting Averages

This then becomes the basis for control charting based upon sample averages or the $\overline{X}$ chart which we got a short glimpse of when we examined how our cup lid molding machine was performing.

The $\overline{X}$ chart is of particular value because it can be used to measure and test any type of variation that is occurring in a process. Items as remote from each other as the following can be measured on this type of chart.

- Lengths
- Pressures
- Temperatures
- On time package delivery
- Return rates from the field
- Average incoming call rate
- On time delivery performance
- Golf scores

It is the work on these types of charts that begins the action on the process to reduce variability. This is the action that is future oriented and leads to improvements in the process.

The sample averages from the $\overline{X}$ charts allow us to observe the following types of changes that can occur in a process.

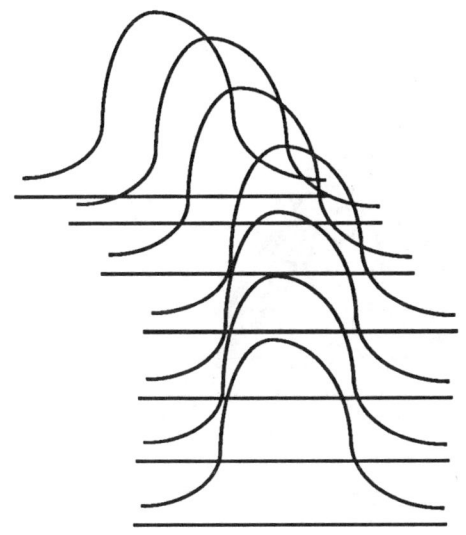

σ′ constant, Sustained shift in $\overline{X}'$

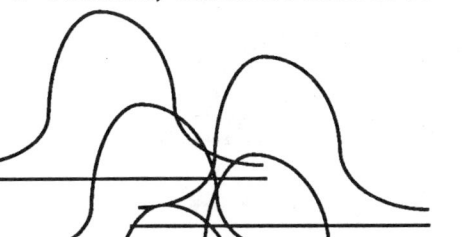

σ′ constant, irregular shift in $\overline{X}'$

161

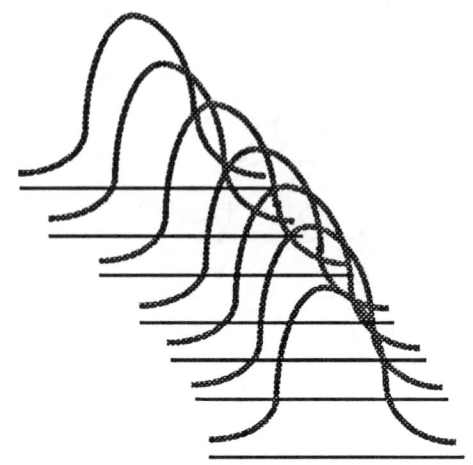

σ' constant, trend in $\overline{X}'$

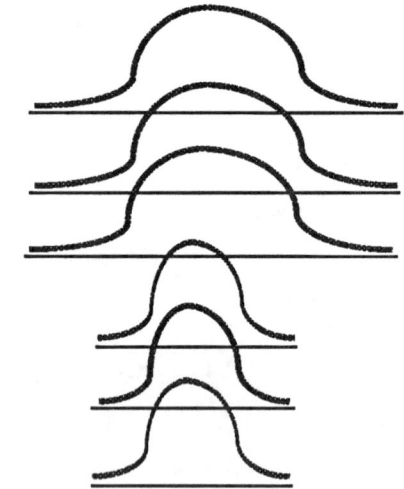

$\overline{X}'$ constant, increase in σ'

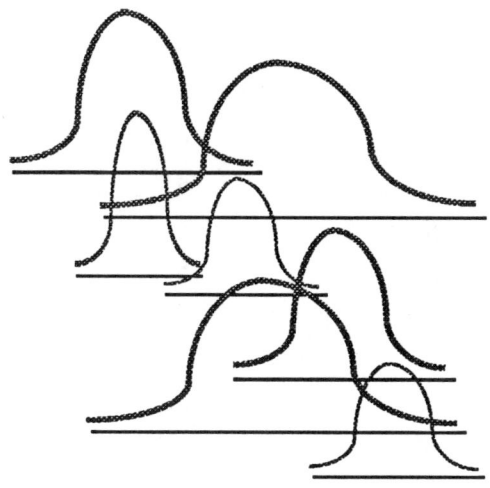

σ' irregular, $\overline{X}'$ irregular

Of these situations, the last is probably the most troublesome as it consists of both common and special causes of variation.

Range Information and the r Chart

In our embroidery operation, we want to measure the consistency of an order where we are sewing in a small six hundred stitch figure on the side panel of a cap. This is a very large order and may repeat again later in the year so we want as clear a picture as possible on how we are doing it.

Each hour we test the run time on five caps. We did this over a five day production period with the following results measured in seconds per cap.

Evaluating the Process

1	2	3	4	5		1	2	3	4	5
54	56	56	56	55		58	57	56	54	54
55	55	55	56	53		51	52	54	56	49
54	52	50	57	55		54	57	54	55	54
56	55	56	53	50		54	53	56	53	55
53	54	57	56	53		53	53	57	54	53
53	50	58	55	54		53	55	57	56	55
53	55	54	55	56		59	54	53	54	55
56	53	53	54	55		54	55	58	55	54
55	52	53	55	55		56	55	55	55	55
50	54	53	55	55		56	55	55	55	55
57	54	53	52	53		54	53	54	55	54
52	52	54	53	55		53	52	55	54	53
54	53	55	52	52		53	52	53	57	53
54	55	54	53	55		53	51	55	50	55
56	53	57	56	54		57	54	56	54	55

There are thirty samples or subgroups of five with the subgroup being read from top to bottom.

164

Subgroup Averages and Embroidery Times

Subgroup	Average	Range	Subgroup	Average	Range
1	55.4	2	16	55.8	4
2	54.8	3	17	52.4	7
3	53.6	7	18	54.8	3
4	54.0	6	19	54.2	3
5	54.4	5	20	54.0	4
6	54.0	8	21	55.2	4
7	54.4	4	22	55.0	6
8	54.2	3	23	55.2	4
9	54.2	4	24	54.8	8
10	53.4	5	25	55.2	1
11	53.8	5	26	54.0	2
12	53.2	3	27	53.4	3
13	53.2	3	28	53.6	5
14	54.2	2	29	52.8	5
15	55.2	4	30	55.2	3

In this process, because the skill of the operator is important, the R chart can be an extremely useful tool for process control. If we find too much dispersion among the operators, the first step in improvement would be to bring that dispersion into statistical control as measured by the R chart,

Evaluating the Process

This principle holds true on all hand operated or operator controlled jobs. We still have our chart of sample means to give information as to how the job is set up but our main sources of variation are likely to be traced to the operator. The variation here is usually of a random nature. An example would be too long a dwell time on one transfer and not enough on another, or erratic performances of all kinds due to a lack of concentration or skill on the part of the individual. These cause an increase in the variability of the output and will be detected by large ranges in the samples taken. It is, thus, the range chart that needs close attention in this instance. It could be regarded as an operator's own personal chart.

Since the value of $\overline{R}$ is used in computing the control limits on the $\overline{X}$ chart, a reduction in the variation on the R chart will result in the tightening of the control limits on the $\overline{X}$ chart as well.

Some causes that can affect the R chart are operator fatigue, a change in the method, a change of operator, or even having different operators (not yet in statistical control) using the same R chart.

Our first step now will be to evaluate the data on an R chart.

Embroidery Time Data Chart

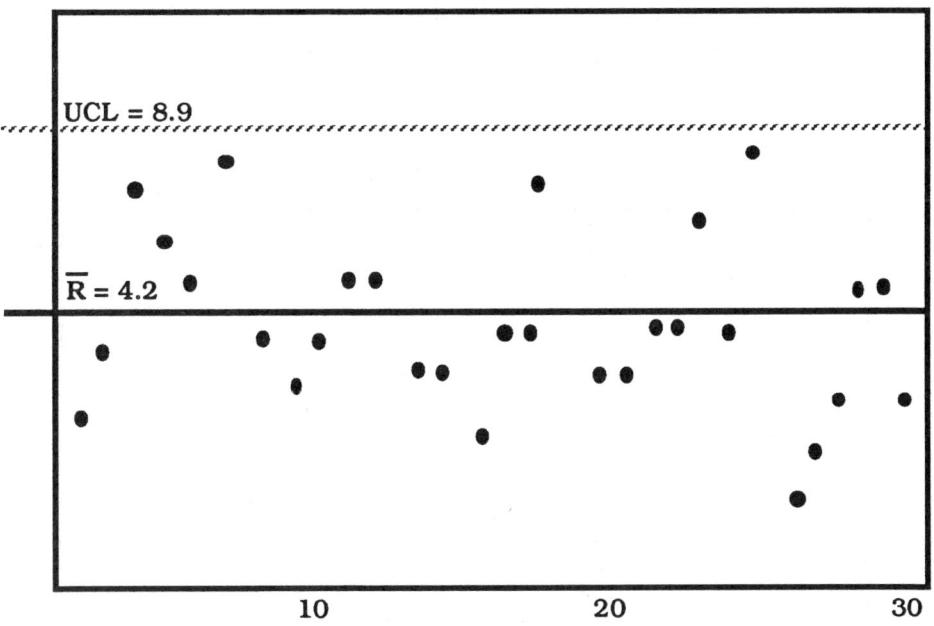

To construct control limits:

Range for each sample = Highest measurement - lowest measurement.

Center Line:

$$\overline{R} = \frac{\text{sum of ranges for samples}}{\text{number of samples}} = \frac{126}{30} = 4.2$$

Upper Control Limit

$$UCL_R = D_4\overline{R} = (2.11)(4.2) = 8.86$$

Lower Control Limit:

$$LCL_R = D_3\overline{R} = (0)(4.2) = \text{no lower limit}$$

Evaluating the Process

Since we are within our control limits and pass both runs tests, we have evidence of statistical control on the ranges. It could then be said that the operators were consistent among themselves with there being no significant differences among them.

We can now go on to the $\overline{X}$ chart.

Embroidery Time Data Chart

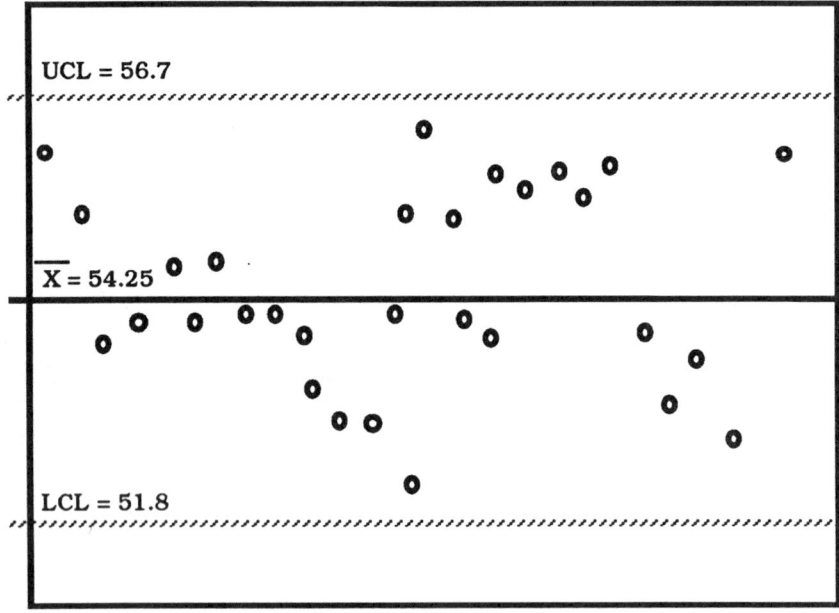

To construct control limits:

$$\overline{X} \text{ for each sample } = \frac{\text{sum of measurements in a sample}}{\text{number of measurements in a sample}}$$

Center Line:

$$\bar{\bar{X}} = \frac{\text{sum of } \bar{X} \text{ values for samples}}{\text{number of samples}} = \frac{1627.6}{30} = 54.2533$$

Upper Control Limit

$$UCL_{\bar{x}} = \bar{\bar{X}} + A_2\bar{R} = 54.2533 + (.58)(4.2) = 56.6893$$

Lower Control Limit:

$$LCL_{\bar{x}} = \bar{\bar{X}} - A_2\bar{R} = 54.2533 - (.58)(4.2) = 51.8173$$

Again, we are within our statistical limits and pass both runs tests. This indicates our embroidery sewing process is in statistical control with respect to the time it is taking to sew up this particular logo.

In addition to having an accurate measurement of the normal embroidery times we have indication that any action to improve these times will require broad based management action on the process because we are seeing only common causes of variation in this process.

Using Estimates

With the process in control with respect to variability, the standard deviation, σ', can be estimated by $\hat{\sigma}'$ where:

$$\hat{\sigma}' = \frac{\bar{R}}{D_2}$$

Evaluating the Process

With the process in control with respect to average, the average time $\overline{X}$, may be estimated by $\overline{\overline{X}}$.

Remember, we are talking about a normal distribution of sample averages, not individual measurements.

We could use the standard normal distribution if we wanted to find out how much of the time we could expect to average 55 seconds or more to do the job.

We use $\overline{\overline{X}}$ to estimate our average $\overline{X}$ and it is 54.2533.

$$\sigma' \text{ is estimated by } \hat{\sigma}' \text{ which is } \frac{\overline{R}}{D_2} = \frac{4.2}{2.326} = 1.806$$

55 seconds is $\dfrac{((55) - (54.2533))}{1.806}$ Or .414 standard deviations above the mean of 54.2533.

From our z table, .3409 or 34.09% of the area under a normal curve or in our case 34.09% of our average sewing times will be 55 seconds (.414 standard deviations) or longer.

The s Chart

Using the standard deviations from each of the samples it is possible to construct an s chart which will tell practically the same story as the R chart. Either one may be used in any case to tell the story. It is not necessary to use both.

R and s (σ) are alternative measures of the same thing that can lead to similar estimates of the standard deviation and similar control limits on the $\overline{X}$ chart.

R is recommended more often in practical control chart work for the simple reasons that it is easier to compute and it is easier to explain. Try explaining the concepts of range to someone and then explain how to compute the standard deviation.

To construct control limits for *s:*

Center Line: $\quad \overline{S} \;=\; \dfrac{\sum s}{K}\quad$ where K is the number of samples and *s* is the standard deviation of each sample.

Upper Control Limit: $\;\; UCL_s \;\; = \;\; B_4 \overline{S}$

Lower Control Limit: $\;\; LCL_s \;\; = \;\; B_3 \overline{S}$

For the $\overline{X}$ chart using *s:* $\hspace{3cm}$ N is the sample size

$$UCL_{\overline{X}} \;\; = \;\; \overline{\overline{X}} \;\; + \;\; 3A_3 s$$

$$LCL_{\overline{X}} \;\; = \;\; \overline{\overline{X}} \;\; - \;\; A_3 s$$

And to estimate the standard deviation from $\overline{s}$:

$$\hat{\sigma} \;\; = \;\; \frac{\overline{S}}{C_4}$$

Process Capability

Estimating the standard deviation becomes important in determining if a process is **capable of meeting specifications.** For the purposes of our discussions we will say the process is capable of doing what it is asked to do if the spread of six standard deviations ($\pm 3\sigma$) can fit within the specification limits.

This would mean that if the process were set up to be centered half way between the specification limits that 99.73% of the output would fall within the specifications.

If the process is not centered or if the natural dispersion of six standard deviations is wider than the specification limits we can use $\hat{\sigma}'$ to estimate how much of the time we will be in and out of specifications.

Some commonly used terms in these types of analyses are:

Engineering tolerance or the distance between (width of) the specification limits and

Natural tolerance or the width of six standard deviations.

Some Examples

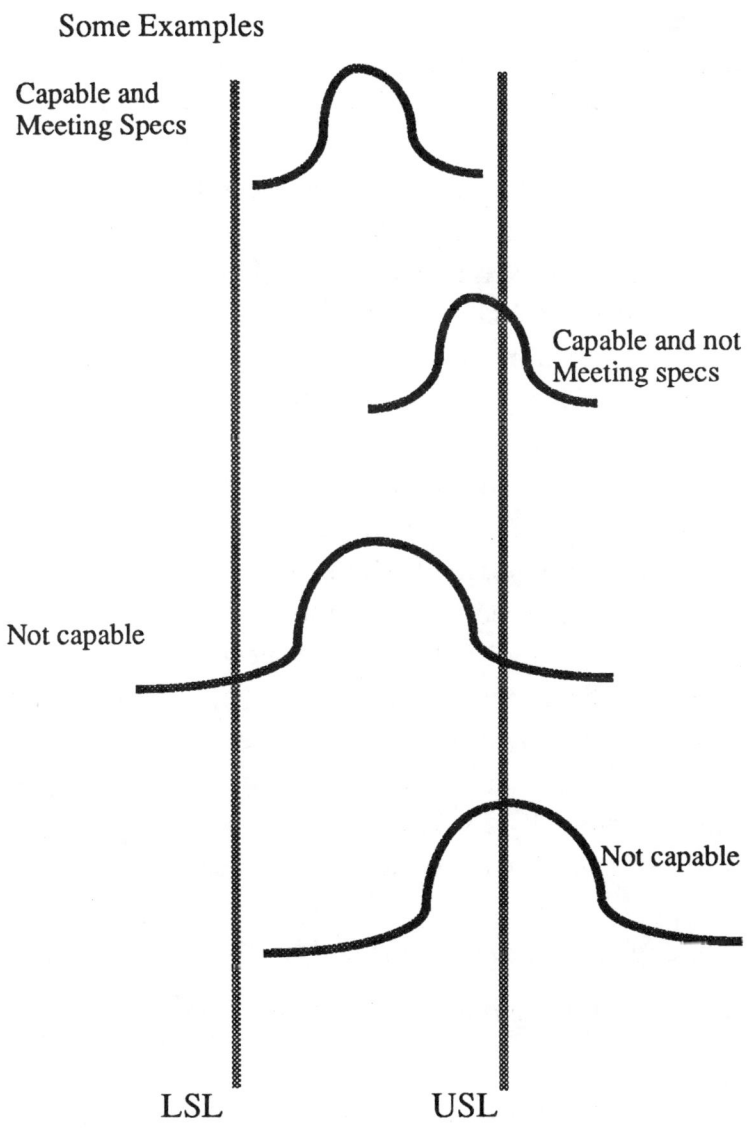

Capable and
Meeting Specs

Capable and not
Meeting specs

Not capable

Not capable

LSL   USL

Evaluating the Process

In an effort to improve a mug decorating process, a lower specification limit on the inside diameter of a coffee mug has been established at 2.77 inches and an upper specification limit has been set at 2.84 inches.

These spec limits were based on the six sigma spread of mugs once received from another factory, the quality of which we would like to see duplicated in our present source.

$\overline{X}$ and R control charts have been initiated at the second factory and have been maintained for fifty samples of five units each with the samples taken from production every two hours. The process appears to be in statistical control with a process average of 2.8017" and a standard deviation of 0.02144".

This factory has set a goal of reducing the variability of the diameter of the mug output to match the quality of the first factory. Until that is accomplished, it is relying on a sorting process to remove the mugs that don't fall within the specification limits.

Based on the information given so far it can arrive at a very close estimate of just how many mugs will have to be sorted out by using this information and the assumption that the diameter measurement is normally distributed.

With $\hat{\sigma}'$ at 0.02144" the natural tolerance is (6)(0.02144) or .1286"

The engineering tolerance is (2.84) - (2.77) or .07 inches.

In standard deviations, that is $\dfrac{0.07}{0.02144}$ = 3.26 standard deviations.

Since the process is centered in the middle of the engineering tolerance, this means that the specification limits are

174

1.63 standard deviations on either side of center. From our normal distribution table we observe that this represents 5.16% of the output at each extreme or 10.32% of the total output that will have to be discarded as not conforming to the size specification until the process can be engineered to as tight a control of variation as factory number one.

$\overline{X}$ and r Chart Review

These charts are used when we have a continuous stream of product or service to be measured. Since it is too tedious and cumbersome to measure everything, we take samples. For example:

Where each point is a unit of output

Evaluating the Process

A sequence of these samples would be tabulated like this.

	$\overline{X}$	r
Sample # 1	$\overline{X}_1$	r_1
Sample # 2	$\overline{X}_2$	r_2
Sample # 3	$\overline{X}_3$	r_3
-	-	-
-	-	-
Sample # K	$\overline{X}_k$	r_k

And we can calculate $\overline{\overline{X}}$ and $\bar{r}$.

Assuming that the process we are measuring is in control we would get a frequency distribution of measurements that might look like this if we measured *every* output from the process.

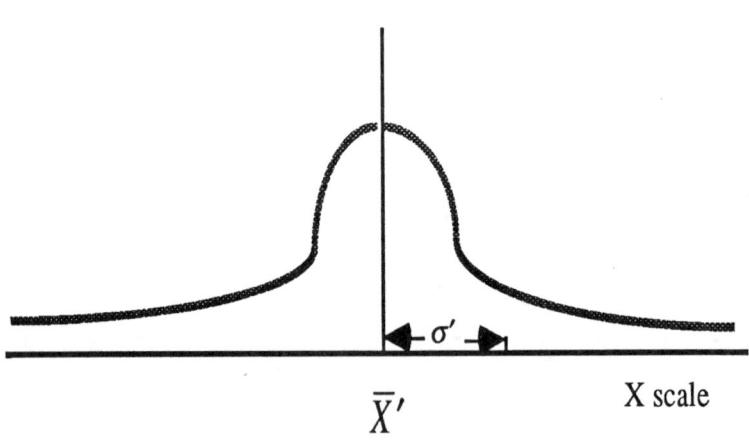

$$\overline{X}'$$ X scale

If the $\overline{X}$ values of *all* possible samples of five were calculated, and arranged according to size, their relative frequencies would look like this:

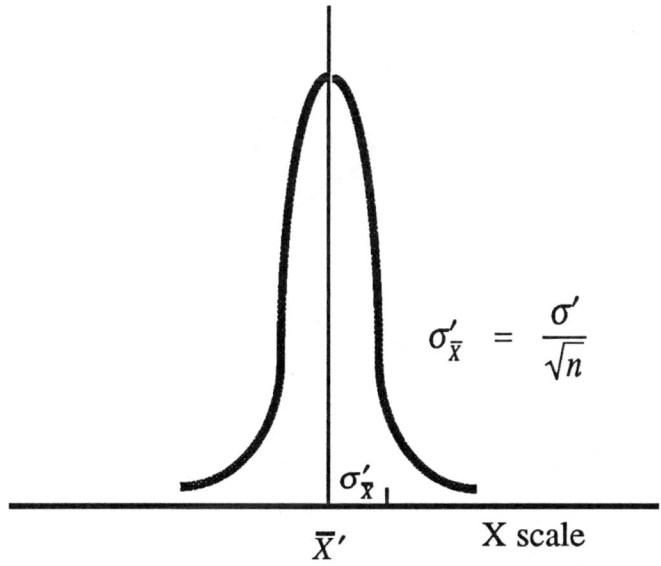

$$\sigma'_{\overline{x}} = \frac{\sigma'}{\sqrt{n}}$$

$\sigma'_{\overline{x}}$

$\overline{X}'$ X scale

This distribution of the sample averages is the basis for the $\overline{X}$ charts and over time looks like this.

177

Evaluating the Process

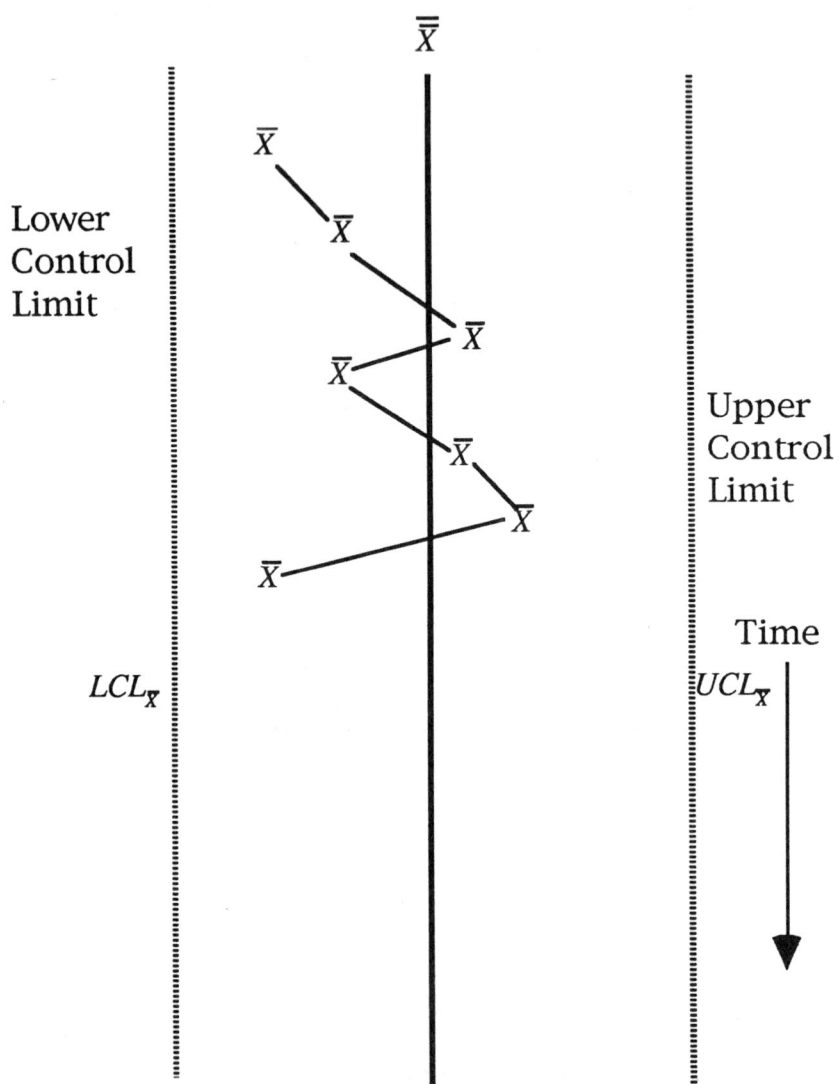

Using the Two Item Moving Range

There is no range as we are used to on any day because a sample of one has the same highest and lowest value. We solve this problem by taking a two - item moving range. That is, take the difference (range) of each two adjacent points.

Then calculate $\bar{r}$ as done previously.

When that is complete, compute;

$$\hat{\sigma}' = \frac{\bar{r}}{d_2} \qquad d_2 \text{ for sample size 2.}$$

Since A_2 is based on the variability of $\overline{X}$ vaules it cannot be used so we use E_2.

$$E_2 = A_2\sqrt{n}$$

so for sample size 2: $\quad E_2 = (1.88)(\sqrt{2}) = 2.66$

The formula for control limits is:

$$\overline{X} \pm E_2\bar{r}$$

and for a two item moving range this becomes $\overline{X} \pm (2.66)\bar{r}$ to yield 3 standard deviation control limits for the X chart.

Let's look at a couple of examples of how this chart might work. First let's look at the on time delivery performance for a company. Here are the results for the last 25 days.

Evaluating the Process

Day	% on time	2 item moving range
1	98	-
2	95	3
3	93	2
4	94	1
5	97	3
6	95	2
7	96	1
8	95	1
9	96	1
10	93	3
11	100	7
12	97	3
13	95	2
14	94	1
15	93	1
16	95	2
17	97	2
18	92	5
19	96	4
20	96	0
21	98	2
22	95	3
23	94	1
24	100	6
25	99	1

$$\overline{X} = 95.7\% \qquad \overline{r} = 2.38$$

First we calculate $\overline{r}$ and determine if the ranges are in statistical control.

$$\overline{r} = \frac{57}{24} = 2.375$$

$$UCL_{\overline{r}} = D_4\overline{r} = (3.267)(2.375) = 7.759$$

$$LCL_{\overline{r}} = D_3\overline{r} = (0)(2.375) = no\ LCL$$

180

All r values fall within the control limits so then plotting the $\overline{X}$ chart we have:

On Time Delivery Performance

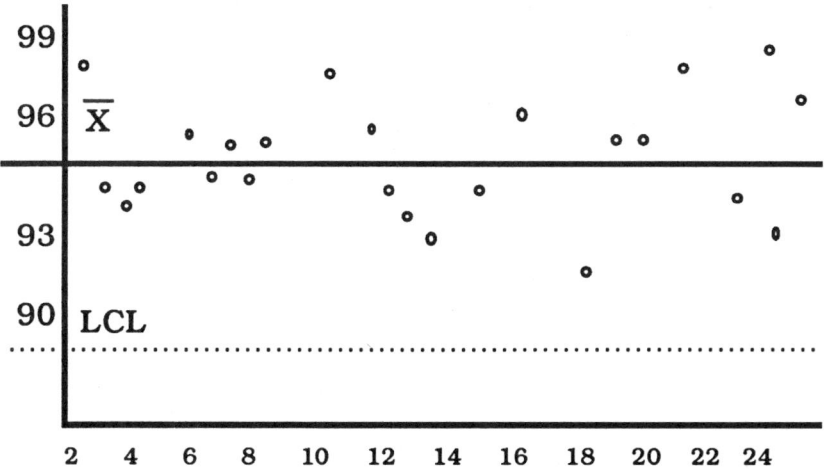

Center Line = 2393/25 = 95.72% on time.

$$\overline{X} \pm 3\sigma$$

For Control Limits;

$$\sigma' = \frac{\bar{r}}{d_2} = \frac{2.375}{1.128} = 2.1055$$

Upper Control Limit:

$$\overline{X} + 3\sigma = 95.72 + (3)(2.106) = \text{over } 100 =$$ no upper limit.

Lower Control Limit:

$$\overline{X} - 3\sigma = 95.72 - (3)(2.106) = 89.3$$

181

Evaluating the Process

We are in statistical control at 95.7% on time delivery.

Charting Costs

A screen department supervisor has decided to monitor the daily payroll cost per screen exposed. The following is the data that was obtained for 25 days.

Day	Payroll Cost/screen	Range
1	2.12	-
2	2.01	.11
3	2.2	.19
4	2.88	.68
5	2.06	.82
6	2.04	.02
7	2.26	.22
8	2.26	.00
9	1.97	.29
10	2.54	.57
11	2.01	.53
12	2.06	.05
13	1.65	.41
14	1.97	.32
15	2.07	.1
16	1.83	.24
17	1.94	.11
18	1.87	.07
19	2.02	.15
20	1.75	.27
21	2.32	.57
22	2.00	.32
23	1.93	.07
24	2.20	.27
25	1.91	.29

Again, we are going to calculate $\bar{r}$ and determine if the ranges are in statistical control.

$$\bar{r} \;=\; \frac{6.67}{24} \;=\; .278$$

$$UCL_r \;=\; D_4\bar{r} \;=\; (3.267)(.278) \;=\; .908$$

$$LCL_r \;=\; D_3\bar{r} \;=\; (0)(.278) \;=\; no\ LCL$$

All values fall within the control limits so we can plot the $\bar{X}$ chart with control limits.

Payroll Cost per Screen

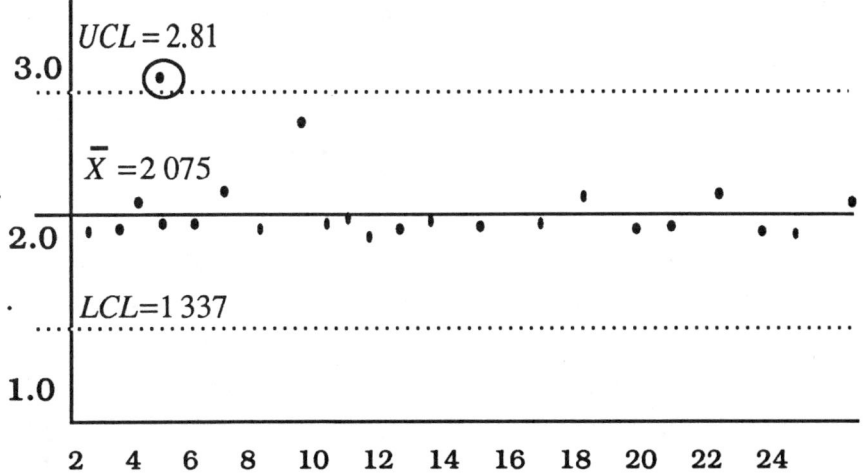

Center Line = 51.87/25 = 2.075 = $\bar{X}$ For Control Limits:

Evaluating the Process

$$\bar{X} \pm 3\sigma$$

$$\hat{\sigma}' = \frac{\bar{r}}{d_2} = \frac{.278}{1.128} = .246$$

$$UCL = \bar{X} + 3\sigma' = 2.075 + (3)(.246) = 2.814$$

$$LCL = \bar{X} - 3\sigma' = 2.075 - (3)(.246) = 1.337$$

Point number four is out of control and would probably warrant investigation. There is a run of ten points but with $l = 18$ and $s = 7$, that falls within our critical value of 12 for length of longest run so we're OK there.

This concludes the description of the types of control charts that are commonly used in assisting in process improvements.

Benefits to Using Control Charts

There are five significant benefits that can be expected when control charts are routinely and correctly used to evaluate processes.

1. The people closest to the operation receive reliable information on when action should be taken and when action should *not* be taken.

2. The effects of changes to the process can be identified through control chart data. (quality improvement, reduced scrap, and increased yield for example.)

3. When a process is in statistical control, performance to specifications will be predictable.

4. The control charts provide a common language from which to discuss performance.

5. Control charts help distinguish special from common causes of variation as a guide to local or management action.

In the next section we will see how to put these charts to use on the shop floor.

Beginning a Charting Program

If history repeats itself,
and the unexpected always happens
How incapable must Man be of learning from experience!

George Bernard Shaw

Setting up the Use of Control Charts

A charting program is used to spread as much information as to what is going on as far out into the company as possible. When people have an abundance of clear information as to what is important and how they are doing in regards to those important values they can make more good decisions that are rational to those values. We just have to get them that information.

In getting started, *do not* attempt to accomplish too much at once. The most important goal in the beginning is to get the fundamental steps down. If you as a manager ask for a pound of charts you will get it and probably very quickly. People as a rule are anxious to please. What you will not get though is the clarity of very thoughtful and reflective information.

Setting up a Charting Program

Trying to start in many areas at once or starting on a very difficult problem only serve to get in the way of the main objective here and that is teaching people how this charting system works.

The first objective to accomplish is to simply get people used to looking at how things are going in a very visual and easy to understand chart form. Of the charts reviewed so far, it is recommended that a simple P chart be used to start.

Go to an area where you are getting some scrap and either on a constant sample size audit basis or on a per shift or per day basis start recording the amount of scrap that is found. At the top of the chart indicate the date or time period covered.

After examination, total everything you looked at and record that as the number inspected. Set aside the defects found and record that as the number rejected. If there are several categories of defective material, now is the time to indicate that. The fraction rejected or percent defective (P) is the number rejected divided by the total number that were looked at.

Set the chart up this way and just let it run for about ten points or days. At this point, the people should be just getting into the habit of recording their data on a regular basis. It is very typical at this stage to have the charts completed at a different time each day and some days are left off because they don't have the time for charting.

Since a good part of this process is behavioral and not statistical, it is important to constantly police these chart activities in the early stages until it becomes an ingrained habit to complete the chartwork in a timely fashion every day. This process just does not work if several days worth of data are accumulated and plotted at the same time. Once you have been doing this for a while it will become apparent why this is so.

Here's the format of a blank P chart.

It is also a good practice to use the back of the chart to display chart interpretation formulas and any checklists that assist in gathering the data. The cost of doing this to have a preprinted chart is minimal compared to how the information will be used.

Here are some samples of the type of information to appear on the back of the chart

P Chart

1. Each point on the Chart = P

2.. The central line on the chart = $\overline{P}$

$$\overline{P} = \frac{\text{The total number of unacceptable items}}{\text{The total number of items inspected}}$$

3. $LCL_p = \overline{P} - 3\sqrt{\dfrac{\overline{P}(1-\overline{P})}{n}}$

4. $UCL_p = \overline{P} + 3\sqrt{\dfrac{\overline{P}(1-\overline{P})}{n}}$

Calculations

1. n = sample size = _____ n

2. Central Line = $\overline{P}$ = _____ $\overline{P}$

3. Lower Control Limit =

$$LCL_{\bar{p}} \quad = \quad \underline{\quad\quad}_{\bar{p}} - 3\sqrt{\frac{\underline{\quad\quad}_{\bar{p}}(1-\underline{\quad\quad}_{\bar{p}})}{\underline{\quad\quad}_{n}}} \quad = \quad \underline{\quad\quad}_{LCL}$$

4. Upper Control Limit =

$$UCL_{\bar{p}} \quad = \quad \underline{\quad\quad}_{\bar{p}} + 3\sqrt{\frac{\underline{\quad\quad}_{\bar{p}}(1-\underline{\quad\quad}_{\bar{p}})}{\underline{\quad\quad}_{n}}} \quad = \quad \underline{\quad\quad}_{UCL}$$

Chart Maintenance

A target that has been used by many in the past was to have the chart updated at the very beginning of the next day, shift, or week. When this is done, those in the group that will pitch in and help solve problems will start taking an interest in this immediate feedback of how they are doing. At this point it is also very realistic and normal to remember that a good number of people will show no interest but will pretend to if you force the issue. That being the case, it's best to accept only the voluntary and genuine interest that arises.

When the chart has been going for a while in this rough stage and people are beginning to show a consistent interest, it is time to begin including more information. By now, some patterns of scrap or defect level should be apparent. Since it is this scrap level we will be trying to improve, we will need more information as to what is going on. Now is the time to begin accumulating the information as to why the scrap is there. A good rule of thumb in the **Pareto** portion of the chart is to list a few main reasons for the defects (not more than eight) and then "other". If the other category gets too big it can be swapped for one of the other eight or the number of categories can be expanded although this is not recommended due to the inherent loss of focus.

It is important to remember that at this stage we are still trying to just fill out our picture of how things are going.

Now let the chart run for another twenty or thirty days on its own. Management staff should be showing an interest in the chart and should insist on its timely posting but that is all at this stage unless it is pointing to a true urgent emergency that will cause the company to fail if not attended to immediately. Again, the most important thing to be accomplished at this stage is to get the information gathering and posting habit so deeply ingrained that it never would occur to them to begin another day, week, or whatever without the chart posted and up to date. During this time, however, some individuals acting on their own initiative will begin solving some of the problems that are popping up. The management goal is to making the tracking habitual. Corrective action will come later.

The next stage at this point will be to calculate the centerline and control limits as was shown earlier. You will need at least twenty points to do this accurately.

What usually pops up at this time is a number of points out of statistical control on the chart. We begin to see how messy the real world can be compared to the theory we covered. The fact of the matter is this is quite normal for the early stages of the charting process.

The special causes (approximately 15 %) of variation that are the resposibility of those closest to the operation stand out right away. A good tool to help deal with these is the corrective action document.

SPC Corrective Action Document

Out of Control Point	Root Cause	Corrective Action	Resp.	Disposition of Material

Each point that is out of control is numbered on the chart and posted on this separate action log which is posted with the chart.

On the log, the root cause of the out of control condition is indicated. We are assuming as a basic rule of thumb that those out of control points indicate special conditions so we will hold those people at the scene responsible for determining the root cause of what happened and initiating corrective action. The corrective action entry on the log then gets filled out.

Some start up problems that are common in what was covered so far is a lack of diligence in keeping the charts up to date and accurate and there will be some fumbling around on the corrective action logs as many people seem to be prone to motherhood and apple pie sort of statements rather than good root cause analysis.

Discipline and persistence come into play to get these initial charts up to a good level of integrity and effective corrective action.

Eventually, these initial charts will settle out and you will find that you have accomplished your first objective. **You will have a clear picture of what is going on.**

Finding the Biggest Problem

When just about all the special causes of variation have been weeded out through local actions on the system as logged on the corrective action documents, a state of statistical control will be reached. There will be a consistent centerline and just about all the points on the chart will fall within the control limits. We have by now created a clear picture of the 85% of the problem that management is responsible for.

Any improvements from here on out will have to be initiated by broad changes to the process that typically go beyond the level of influence of people at the local level.

The effects of any change will also have to be measured using some of the statistical signals covered earlier. Quick judgements after looking at a few numbers are not only inappropriate, they may be misleading.

The next step after the achievement of statistical control and acquiring a clear picture of how things are going is to get a clear picture of what the biggest problem is. We need this because of time constraints.

If we have the time and resources to spend on every problem we are faced with, chances are we have too many people on the payroll and are spending too much. The reality is that in improving processes we have only limited resources to spend on solving the problem. To keep from squandering those resources we want to make sure we are addressing our biggest problem.

There are some problems here, particularly among individuals or groups that are relatively inexperienced, where they think all problems are important and either want to work on too many at once or they want to elevate small problems to "big" status.

Another situation may be that someone's big problem may be one of the smaller issues we are faced with as an overall organization. In order to work on what is truly the most important issue, their problem may have to be put on the back burner much to their dismay.

We use the Pareto analysis as a frame of reference then to provide guidance. We want to know what our biggest problem is.

We may not work on it, though in just about all cases it will get our priority attention.

There may be some cases where we will elect to move past our biggest problem onto something else but we only want to do that when everyone clearly understands we are bypassing our biggest problem in order to do this. This picture also helps us restrain ourselves from exercising poor judgement.

There are those who like to swat flies. A Pareto will tell us that while we are swatting flies, there is still a lion creeping up behind us.

By now, we have a clear picture of what is going on from our regular and accurate charting efforts. We know that once we are in statistical control (with a few exceptions) we are unlikely to see process improvements unless we begin to take broad action on the system and we know what our biggest problem is.

Root Cause Analysis

If we work on our biggest problem first we can assume most of the time that that will yield the greatest reward for our efforts. We are now ready to begin some broad based actions on the system.

To do that we need to assemble a group of people with a good technical understanding of our situation and a desire to solve the problem. Since we are probably going to have to take broad based action on the system to solve our problem, this group should be broad based in their levels of expertise. The common denominator for all is they are each very close to the situation at hand. We are not going to be after abstract theories here. We will require a high degree of first hand knowledge.

Once the group is assembled we are going to use a series of tightly focused meetings to go after the problem and find a solution.

The Fishbone

The first thing they will do with the information so far is place the number one problem at the focal point of a cause and effect diagram. (also called a fishbone diagram) An example of a fishbone is shown in the diagram that follows. As you can see from the example, it resembles the skeleton of a fish, hence the name.

Using the fishbone is not an exercise to be filled out by an individual. It is a way to help structure the thinking of the group that is trying to analyze the number one problem it is facing. The problem that shows up as number on in the Pareto analysis gets listed as the effect to be analyzed.

The group that management gets together to go after this problem then looks at what could be wrong with the machinery, methods, people. materials, and sometimes the environment that could cause this problem.

The trick to making this work is to ask the question why? a few times for each of the causes being investigated. For many, this alone is quite a deviation from the old standard of asking "who screwed up?" one time.

For example:

The number one problem for the plant last week was off register printing.

Why? (#1) - Most of the problems seem to be coming from press #4.

Why? (#2) - The second color down can't hold register.

Why? (#3) - The bearing race on the drive side is shot.

Why? (#4) - Because it is receiving insufficient lubrication during the monthly P.M.

Why? (#5) - Because the grease fitting does not have sufficient capacity for the lubrication required.

Solution: Redesign the lubrication system for the drive side of press #4.

The same questioning process is followed for each of the causes (m's). As each "why" is answered, another bone is put on the fish. When we are done, the more bones we have on the fish, the better job we did of picking apart the problem.

Fishbone Chart or Cause and Effect Diagram

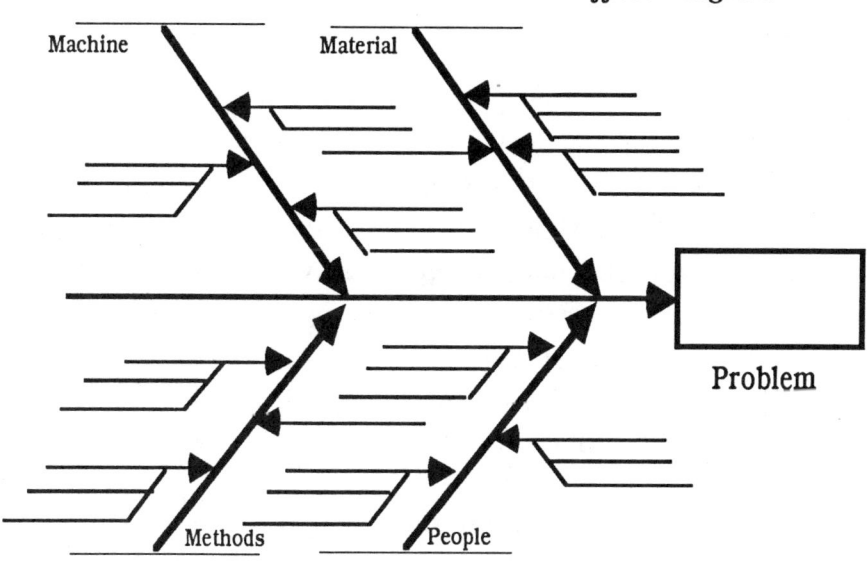

This activity has to take place in the right kind of collaborative atmosphere. It is a way to help structure group thinking. It is not an exercise in paperwork. If one person just sits down and fills one out, you may get a very neat and professional looking fishbone but you will lose the impact of the group. If you want the forms to look good, you have done a good job. If you wanted to get results and show continuous improvement, you probably weren't effective.

Organizing Action Teams to Solve Problems

When a small company starts out, it is usually dependent on one individual at the very beginning at least to come up with the answers to all the problems it is faced with. To be successful, that person has to come up with good answers. As the company evolves, that person becomes a small group of key individuals who are expected to come up with the solutions to a somewhat larger number of problem situations, and again, a good deal of the success that company can expect is directly tied in to how good their responses are.

There comes a point in time though where a company or department becomes so large that it just becomes too inefficient to attempt to solve all the problems from the top. The management responsibility changes from coming up with good answers to establishing the tools necessary to insure that the group itself is organized and trained in such a fashion that it can function effectively in solving these problems. Organizing action teams is one of these tools.

One of the first steps in effective problem solving is the distillation of a list of many problems that seems unmanageable due to its size down to the top two or three problems the group is faced with. If the chart evidence has not been collected or is not available, a good first step is to get the group assembled and have them compile a list of the problem areas they should work on.

After that list is put together, each person should independently indicate the top three issues that should be looked at first. When that is done by everyone, the list should now be narrowed down to four or five items that recieved most of the votes.

In attacking the list of problems in this manner, the group tends to indicte those areas that everyone is having a problem with. In the procsess, those areas that only a few people are having problems with and those people who are having problems with everything are weeded out.

This, by the way, is not necessarily a cruel step. In these types of individual cases, the best approach to improved performance is individual coaching and counseling. Since those approaches are beyond the scope of a group called together to work on a problem with the overall system, it is appropriate to cut those areas out so the group can focus on more global problem areas where it is most likely to be more effective.

Once the group has reached a consensus of the first two or three areas to be attacked, action teams are then organized to begin this task.

As with the startup of the charting program, patience is again the key requirement for continuing success. It is best to begin with just one action team organized to attack a fairly straightforward problem. It just works better if they have some practice in going through the steps of effective problem solving and gain that experience before they are thrown at some really messy situation.

If the main group or department is large enough to begin more than one action team project, it may work better if the second project starts two weeks or so after the first and so forth with any other action teams. This allows the group leader to focus whatever time there is available on each team in its critical beginning phases.

There are six steps the action teams will follow.

1. Organize the team and select a leader.
2. The team meets, analyzes the situation, and comes up with preliminary recommendations.
3. These recommendations are presented to the group as a whole for comment and feedback.
4. The team reconvenes to make any required changes to their plan based on this feedback.
5. The team makes its final presentation to management.
6. Management considers these recommendations and makes the final presentation to the group as to what specific action steps will be taken based upon the groups recommendations.

While all this is going on, it may be necessary for the team to spin off subgroups to investigate specific portions of the problem or call in expert help if they get stumped in an area. It is quite common for this process to take a few weeks and several meetings to properly address a problem area.

The Problem Analysis Meeting

From this stage on in the charting program, the technique of the charts, mathematics, etc. is not nearly as important as how the group functions. The success of this portion of the process rests with the qualities of leadership and group dynamics.

Highly focused and skillfully managed problem solving meetings are needed in order to be effective here.

First, let's review how information flows in meetings and what type of flow we are looking for in a problem solving meeting.

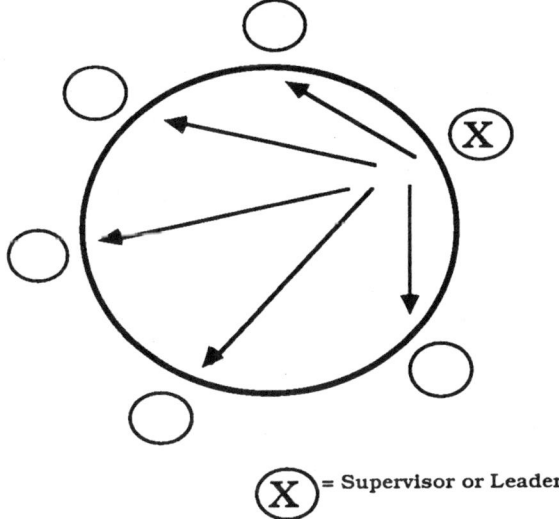

$\widehat{X}$ = Supervisor or Leader

In this first type of meeting the information is flowing from the leader to the others. This is a good format for instructing, giving out information, or dealing with a situation that has to be handled quickly. i.e......................FIRE!!!!!!!!!!!!!

Although there are times when this type of meeting is very appropriate, it is not an effective style for a problem solving meeting. Since only one person is doing most of the talking and since the information is going only one way, the kind of information we are seeking is not surfacing. Since that is a key group dynamic for effective problem solving, we would have a relatively low expectation of anything worthwhile coming out of a problem solving meeting run in this fashion.

Some caution people to lower their expectations if they find themselves in a problem solving meeting like this. The problem solving process still works, it's just that they will be unlikely to see strong results due to the type of meeting they used.

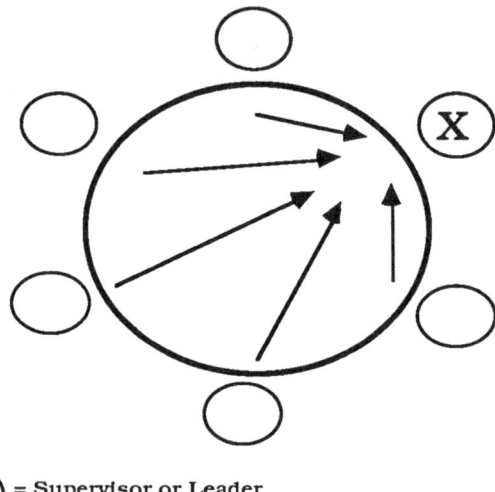

$\left(\textbf{X}\right)$ = Supervisor or Leader

Here is another type of meeting that can serve a useful purpose depending upon the circumstances. This format is great for a gripe session. Periodic sessions like these are necessary because they help clear the air of festering problems.

Everyone gets a chance to speak up and get their grievances off their chest. The purpose of the meeting is to let whatever is bothering anyone flow out so the leader just listens and makes note of what is said. The only exception would be to clarify some points. Since feedback on the part of the leader would slow down that flow it is not given during that meeting. It will come later.

Right now, the leader is just listening, understanding, questioning to clarify, and noting everything that is being brought up.

If these meetings don't occur regularly or if there are insufficient channels of communication to raise grievances, an early problem solving meeting can easily slip into this format on its own.

There is a catharsis on the part of the group and a hidden agenda of unaired grievances just explodes onto the table.

Again, if this happens, deal with it as best you can recognizing that the effectiveness of the intended problem solving probably won't be as high as it could be.

This is the type of problem solving dynamic we are striving for.

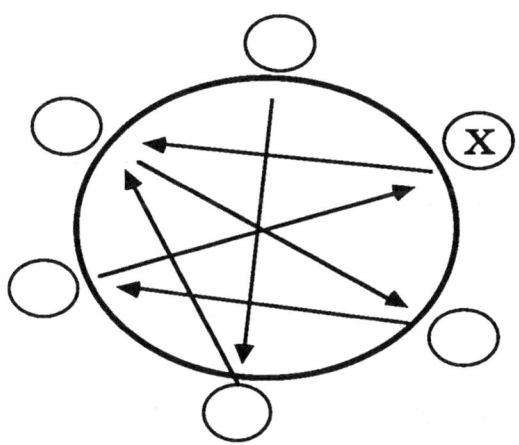

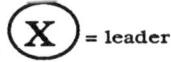 = leader

Here everyone is a peer with regards to the information flow. It is not coming from or going to anyone in particular. It is interactive and commonly shared. When this happens in a company, problems get solved and companies not only survive, they prosper.

Leader Characteristics

It takes work and understanding on the part of the leader to get to this level of performance though.

First, leaders have to be on good terms with themselves with a good level of self knowledge and understanding. There is a need to understand *personal* reactions to all the different situations they are faced with.

Secondly, if the leader has communicated other organizational matters directly and frequently, there will be no need to do that in this meeting, hence no disruptions or distractions.

Lastly, if the group has had continuous access to effective grievance communication channels there will be no need to bring them up here as part of a hidden agenda.

Problem Solving Guidelines

Here are some guidelines on how to get your problem solving meetings up onto an effective plane.

• Set clear objectives for the meeting. Before you begin the meeting, write down your objectives. Make sure these are presented clearly to the group. Ask for feedback. Everyone present should know what your goals are for the meeting.

- Provide structure and context for everyone there. This includes a review of where you came from, what the problems have been, and where the company is now in relation to these problems. A review of the P chart, Pareto, and the fishbone provides good context. The fishbone should correspond to the meeting's objectives.

- Encourage participation by all members. This task falls upon the leader to encourage participation from all members of the group because without it, your chances of coming to terms with the problems you are faced with will be severely diminished.

- Keep the meeting focused on the task. The people in the meeting have diverse interests and many different problems of their own. In addition, so many issues are interconnected that it will take some hard work on the part of the leader to keep the meeting on track. Hidden agendas that emerge here must be set aside to other meetings in order to keep this one on track.

- Summarize decisions and agreements. Be sure to summarize and note all decisions and agreements that the group reaches in the meeting. Failing to do this will cause most of the meeting's work to be wasted.

- Set followup dates and clarify responsibilities of everyone there. This will insure that the decisions arrived at in the meeting will be carried out.

- Post the minutes or other summary of the meeting right up onto the visual area where the charting, Pareto, and fishbone are posted. This begins to invoke a sense of closure and resolution to the problem and it communicates that things are really being done.

Plans for Action

Now that you have come this far in the charting process you are ready to get some solutions going for your largest problems. In selecting a solution you will be looking for something that will solve all or part of the problem permanently.

For it to make sense, the benefits will have to be worth the time, cost, and effort spent. It may even be necessary to formally spell out the benefits in a cost/benefit analysis to evaluate the impact of the proposed solution. The solution will need all the support necessary to make the implementation successful.

Once the solution is selected, a plan for its implementation will have to be created. This plan should outline any necessary modification or changes to the process and the development of or changes to any standard operating procedures. A specific action plan for putting the solution into operation will also have to be created. This action plan will list each action item, who is going to do it, when it will be done, and a feedback mechanism to check off when it is completed or to update how the implementation is going.

This plan of action should be posted up with the other charting activity. It is actually better if it can be condensed enough and still be understood to write in the action steps right on the original chart. Remember, there are no points for chart neatness just as there should be little emphasis on the number of charts. The test of the effectiveness of this activity is the *actual results*.

208

A chart with a long history and many notes written on it will offer more clarity to someone than a neatly displayed chart with no other information on it.

You will know you have completed this part of the charting process when you have selected a solution. If you have resisted the temptation of the quick solution and have systematicaly gathered and analyzed the data using statistical methods you will be in a position to develop a solution that can really eliminate all or part of the problem permanently.

The Cost/Benefit Analysis

The cost/benefit analysis should be used at this point if the implementation requires significant cost. You just don't think up great ideas and run out to spend money. We simply have to know if the benefits we expect are worth the cost of what we will spend.

For example:

We want to increase the sales revenue of the cap line by offering a customer's own label in a cap. We feel that if we can offer that we can generate an additional $50,000 a year in addditional business.

Costs		Benefits	
Machine;	$8,000	$50,000 sales @ 25% margin	
Labels; 25,000@ .02 ea =	500		
Labor to sew @ .02 ea =	500	=(50,000)(.25) = $12,500	
thread	50		
total costs =	$9,050	total benefits =	$12,500

The ratio of benefits to costs is $\dfrac{12,500}{9,050}$ or a \$1.38 return on every dollar spent. This plus other benefits such as broadening the base of services to the customer and building a reputation for broad service should be enough to justify a go ahead with this plan.

The Charting Cycle

It's a continuous flow process that follows this cycle.

1. How are we doing?
2. What's our biggest problem?
3. Let's pick it apart.
4. Effective group dynamics are key.
5. Here's our plan of action.
6. Here's our record of what we tried and when.

Looking at a flow diagram of this charting process:

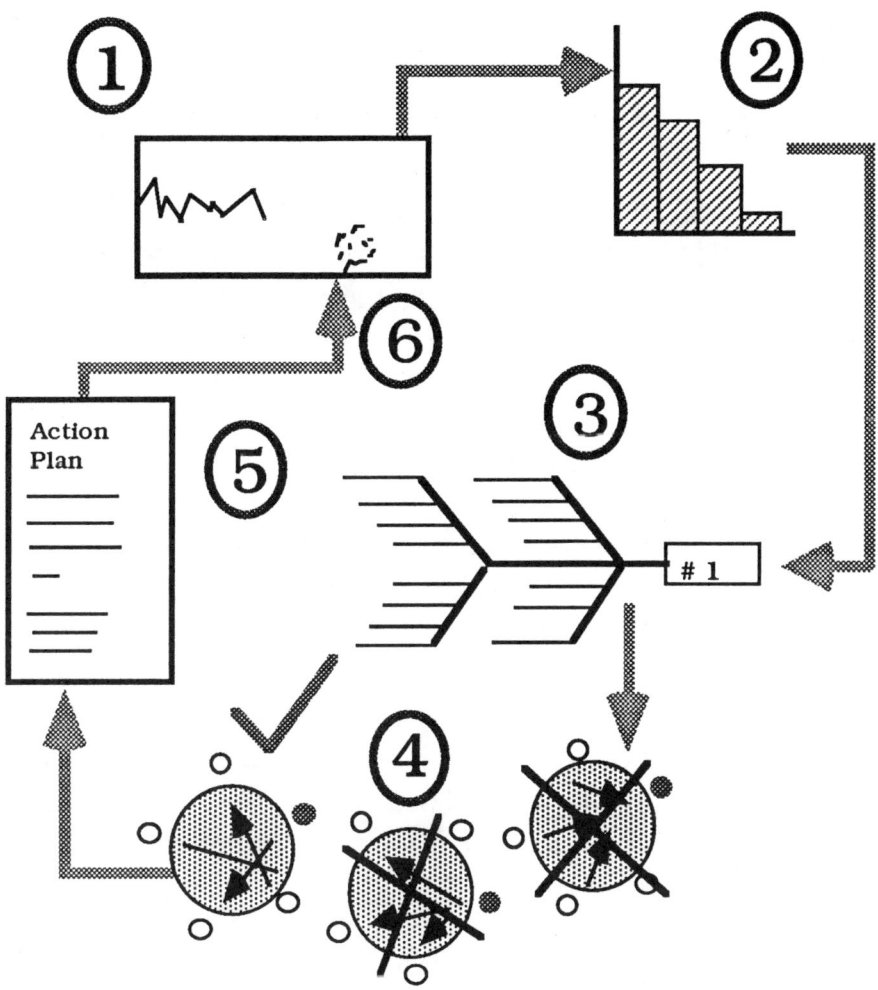

That was a charting program for working on the output of the process. Since that deals with history, we haven't made the process better but we sure have more information as to how it is doing. To make improvements to the process you have to work on the process itself. The charting approach follows the same basic principles but the charts are different.

Process Improvements With the Charting Cycle

To begin with, we are going to use some form of $\overline{X}$ chart. We are going to be measuring variables data where before we were measuring attributes data. Although $\overline{X}$ and r and $\overline{X}$ and s charts were covered in good detail earlier, an example of the $\overline{X}$ and r chart format is shown in figure 4. Also shown is the type of instructive information that can be preprinted on the back of the blank chart to assist those who use it.

When this type of chart is up and running, we will go to the Pareto analysis next. Now rather than asking what our biggest problem is we will be determining our largest source of variation.

From the Pareto to the fishbone to the group dynamics to the action plan the activities of the group working on this are the same as described earlier. The only difference is now we are looking to reduce causes of variation and our resulting action plan will be something that reduces variation.

In this format, the $\overline{X}$ and r charts are both on the same page.

Figure 4

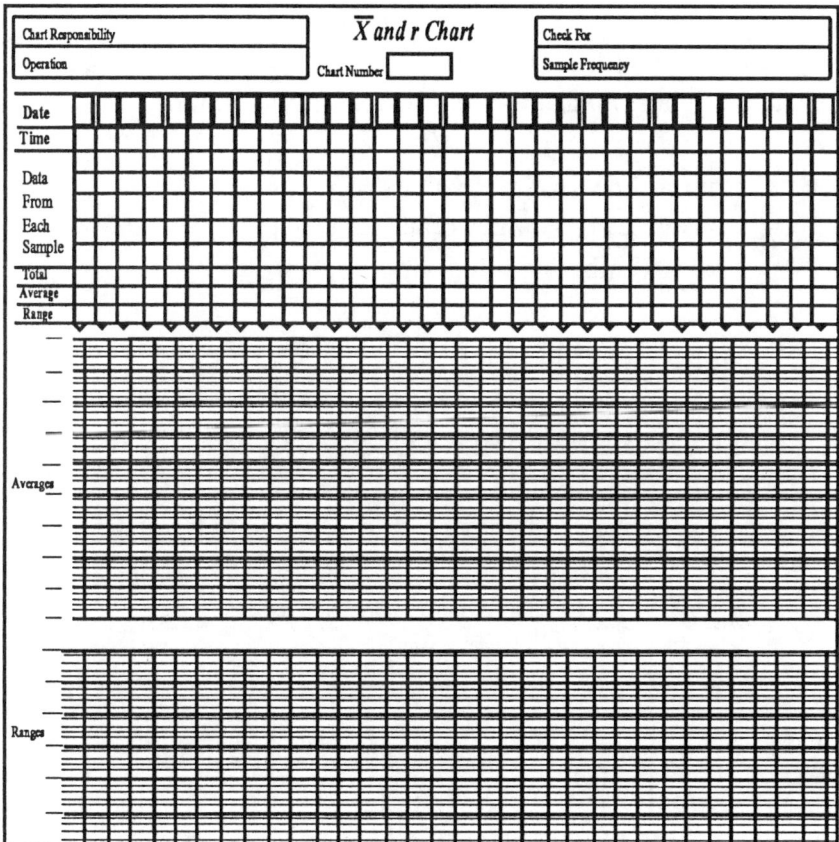

The information on the back of the chart provides a ready reference to those who are using it.

R Chart

1. Each point = R (Range)

R = Highest measurement - lowest measurement

2. Central line of the R values = $\bar{R}$

$$\bar{R} = \frac{\text{Sum of the ranges of all subgroups}}{\text{Number of subgroup samples}}$$

3. Upper Control Limit = $UCL_{\bar{R}}$ = $D_4 (\bar{R})$

4. Lower Control Limit = $LCL_{\bar{R}}$ = $D_3 (\bar{R})$

n =	2	3	4	5	6	7
D_3						.08
D_4	3.27	2.57	2.28	2.11	2.00	1.92

$\bar{X}$ Chart

1. Each point = $\bar{X}$ (the average of the subgroup)
2. Central line of the $\bar{X}$ values = $\bar{\bar{X}}$

$$\bar{\bar{X}} = \frac{\text{Sum of the ranges of all subgroups}}{\text{Number of Subgroup Samples}}$$

3. Upper Control Limit = $UCL_{\bar{X}}$ = $\bar{\bar{X}} + A_2 (\bar{R})$

4. Lower Control Limit = $LCL_{\bar{X}}$ = $\bar{\bar{X}} - A_2 (\bar{R})$

n =	2	3	4	5	6	7
A_2	1.88	1.02	.73	.58	.48	.42

n = sample size

214

The charting process using $\overline{X}$ and r charts

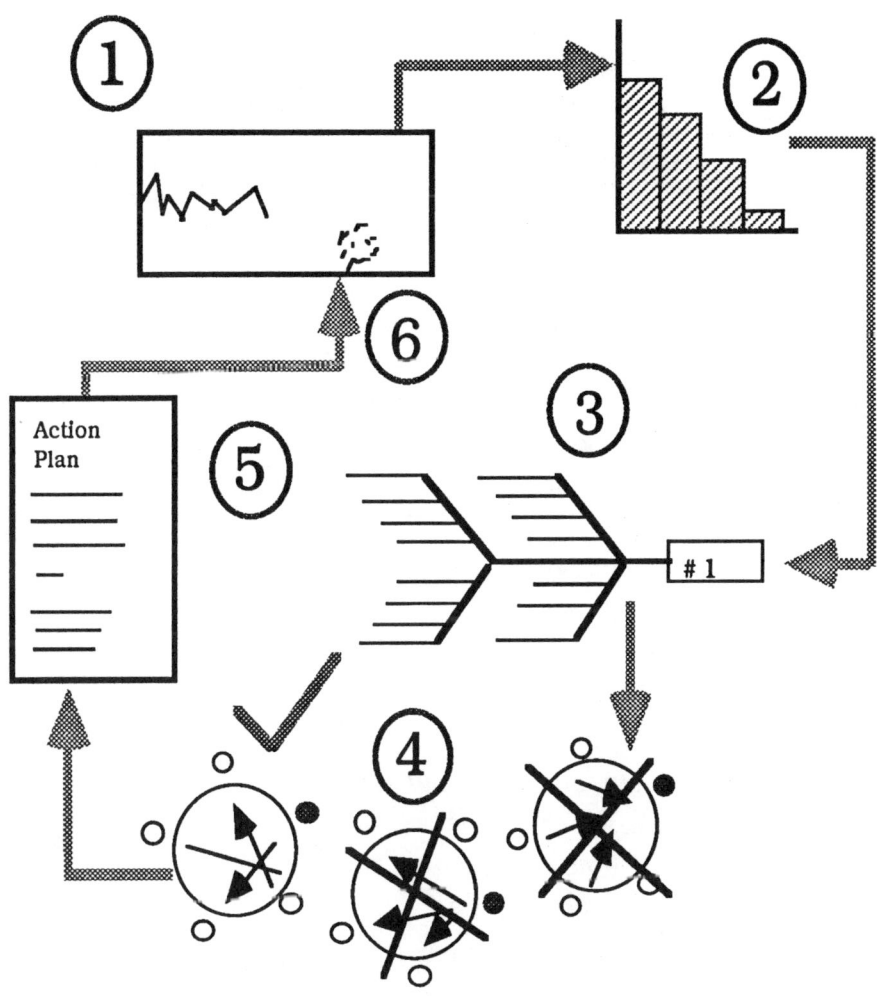

Setting up a Charting Program

The Sequence in the thought pattern shown in the diagram is as follows.

1. What variation are we experiencing?
2. What is the biggest source of variation?
3. Why it it?
4. Effective group dynamics are necessary?
5. Here's a plan to reduce this source of variation?
6. Here's a record of what we tried and when.?

Once the charting program has been underway for a while using the charts we just covered, it can be expanded into just about any area.

Some unique but effective areas could include:

- Safety performance
- Lead times
- Inventory accuracy
- % Budget adherence
- Incoming phone call activity
- Outgoing phone call activity
- Customer ratings
- On time delivery
- Levels of returns
- Sales calls per time period
- Return on net assets
- New product performance
- Forecast accuracy

The Spider Chart

A spider chart is a good tool to provide a snapshot of the status of several different charts or activities. It gets the information from several areas onto one spot and shows it in a way that measures overall performance. The plots of each of the points brought over from another chart are plotted on one of the many axes. Good performance is closer to the center and poor performance is on the edge. After all the points are plotted, they are connected to form an area in the center. The smaller the enclosed area, the better the overall performance.

As an example:

Overall Performance

Data:

On time Delivery	96%
Returns & allowances	1.8%
Lead time (days)	5
Inventory turns	3.5
Scrap	1.1%
Customer evaluation	3.5

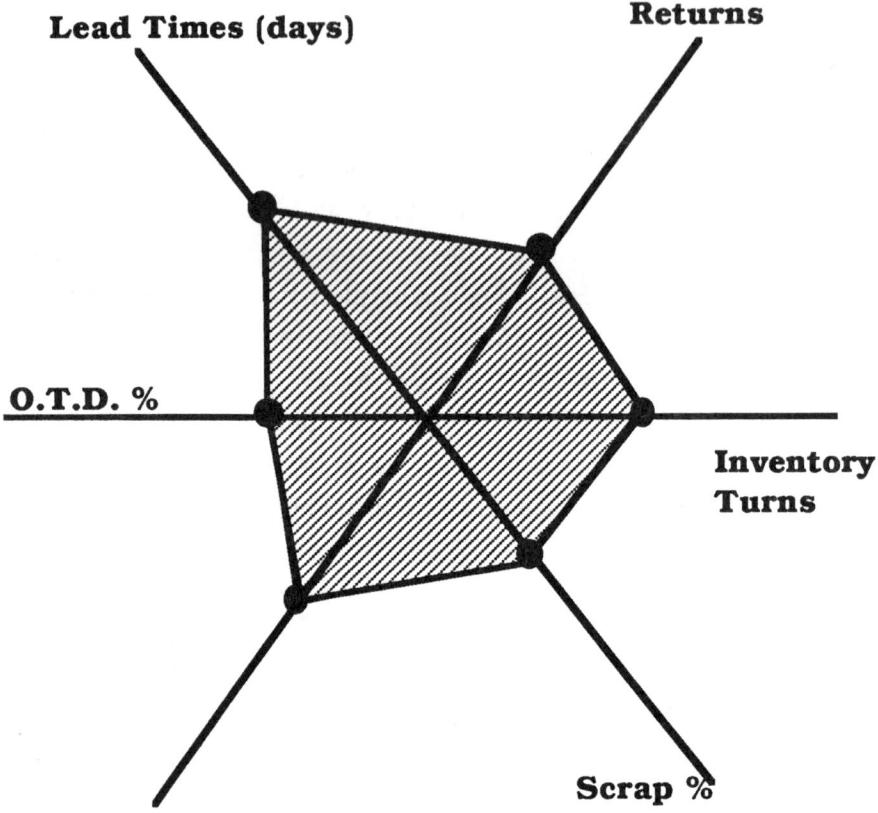

Lead Times (days)

Returns

O.T.D. %

Inventory Turns

Scrap %

Customer Evaluations

This chart is good for showing several areas at once. The smaller the enclosed area, the better the performance.

Summary

In summary, there are four key points to remember when starting and running a charting program.

1. Begin with a small and manageable project. Let everyone first see how this process works with one good example. Although it may seem like nothing is happening at the time, attempting too much at once is a sure ticket to failure.

2. Let the project run on its own. Do not try to rush it. Again, there are more failures from lack of patience than lack of effort.

3. Get the group dynamics right. This may require some additional training in this area before beginning a charting program but a dysfunctional group will not accomplish much.

4. Let everyone see how it's going. Make the feedback;

    a. immediate
    b. easy to understand
    c. visible for all to see.

Do all this and down the road you will begin to see visible and permanent improvements in performance.

Chart Interpretation and Advanced Techniques

We should be careful to get out of an experience only the wisdom that is in it - and stop there; lest we be like the cat that sit down on a hot stove-lid. She will never sit down on a hot stove-lid again - and that is well; but she will also never sit down on a cold one anymore.

Mark Twain

After a general charting program has been set and the disciplines have been practiced for long enough that they have become habit, it is time to move on to more sophisticated charting and interpretation methods. The following is a brief overview of some of those techniques using real examples from the shop floor.

Engineering Tolerances

One our products consists of a plastic lid that fits in the top of a plastic cup. From what we have learned about processes that produce things like cups and lids, we know we will have variation in the inside diameter of the cup and the outside diameter of the lid.

With that variation occurring, how do we prevent getting a fit so tight that the lid won't go on or so loose that hot coffee may spill out onto a user. Here is a simple example of how our next example works.

Lets suppose that all of the possible cup diameters are either 6,7, or 8, in equal proportions. After a very large number of cups are collected and measured, we calculate their average and standard deviation.

$$X_1 = \text{each recorded value}$$

$$\overline{X_1}' = \frac{6+7+8}{3} = 7$$

$$\sigma_1' = \frac{\sqrt{(6-\overline{X})^2 + (7-\overline{X})^2 + (8-\overline{X})^2}}{3} = \frac{\sqrt{2}}{3} = \sqrt{.67} = .8165$$

The variance $= \sigma_1'^2 = (.8165)^2 = .67$

Now lets suppose that all possible lid diameters are 2,3, or 4, in equal proportions. A very large number of lids are collected and measured and we calculate their average and standard deviation.

$$X_2 = \text{each recorded value.}$$

$$\overline{X}_2 = \frac{2+3+4}{3} = 3$$

$$\sigma_2' = \sqrt{\frac{(2-3)^2 + (3-3)^2 + (4-3)^2}{3}} = .8165$$

The variance = $\sigma_2'^2 = (.8165)^2 = .67$

Now suppose that cups and lids are selected at random coming out of each of their respective molding machines. The possible combination of cups and lids we could find would be as follows.

X_1 = cups
X_2 = Lids

X_1	X_2
6	2
6	3
6	4
7	2
7	3
7	4
8	2
8	3
8	4

Since it is the fit between these two parts we are interested in, we will measure the distance between X_1 and X_2 and call it z.

$$z = X_1 - X_2$$

X_1	X_2	$z = X_1 - X_2$
6	2	4
6	3	3
6	4	2
7	2	5
7	3	4
7	4	3
8	2	6
8	3	5
8	4	4

These nine values of z would occur with roughly equal frequency since the combinations of X_1 and X_2 will occur with roughly equal frequency. After a large number of values of z are recorded, we will see another distribution with its own average and standard deviation.

$$\bar{Z}' = \bar{X}_1 - \bar{X}_2 = 7 - 3 = 4$$

variance: $\sigma_z'^2 = \sigma_1'^2 + \sigma_2'^2 = .6667 + .667 + 1.3333$

standard deviation: $\sigma_z' = \sqrt{\sigma_z'} = \sqrt{1.3333} = 1.1547$

Here is a histogram of these possible combinations

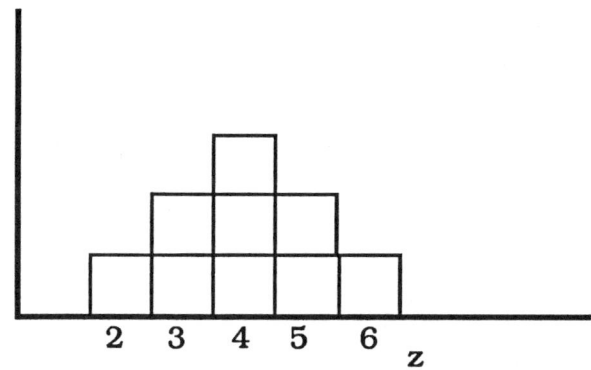

With this information available in this fashion, this distribution can be compared with any specification limits which would show at what value the fit is too loose and when the fit is too tight.

Averages From Two Processes

Now let's look at this same problem with real and not so simple numbers. The important dimensions of the plastic cup assembly are the inside dimension of the cup, X_i, and the outside dimension of the lid, X_o, since these two dimensions determine the clearance, X_c of these two components in the assembly

Extensive work was done, including field surveys, to determine the maximum and minimum clearances to assure proper

Chart Analysis

function in use. It was determined that the clearance should be no less than .004 millimeters and no greater than .015 millimeters. Therefore, a clearance specification of .0095 ± .0055mm was written.

A study of current production of the two components was made with the following results.

cups:

$$\overline{\overline{X}}_i = 5.0120mm \qquad\qquad \hat{\sigma}'_i = .0010 \qquad normal\ distribution$$

lids:

$$\overline{\overline{X}}_o = 5.0005mm \qquad\qquad \hat{\sigma}'_o = .0015 \qquad normal\ distribution$$

Average

clearance: $\overline{X}_c = \overline{\overline{X}}_i - \overline{\overline{X}}_o = (5.0120 - 5.0005) \quad = \quad .0115$

Variance of clearance:

$$\sigma'^2_c = \sigma'^2_i + \sigma'^2_o = (.001)^2 + (.0015)^2 = .00000325$$

Standard Deviation of Clearance:

$$\sigma'_c = \sqrt{\sigma'^2_c} = \sqrt{.00000325} = .0018$$

Set in a table we have:

Item	Value	Mean	Std Dev	Variance	Specs
cup I.D.	X_i	5.0120	.001	.000001	N/A
lid O.D.	X_o	5.0005	.0015	.0000022	N/A
clearance	X_c	.0115	.0018	.0000032	.0095 ± .0055

Using the Normal Curve

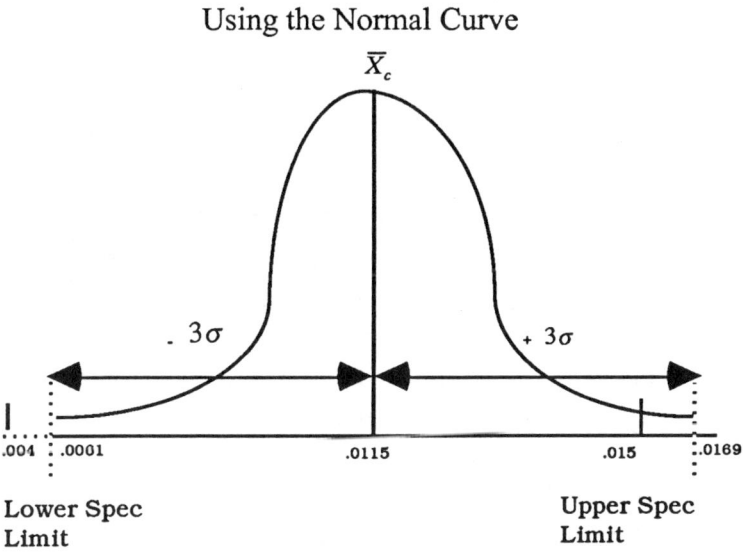

The engineering tolerance = ± .0055 = (2)(.0055) = .011

The natural tolerance = $(6)(\sigma') = (6)(.0018) = .0108$ therefore the process is capable of achieving the specifications because .0108 fits within the .011 boundaries or specifications.

The smallest expected clearance (-3 σ) is .0061 which is larger than the minimum specification so none of the lids will be too tight as defined by the engineering specification.

The largest expected clearance (+3 σ) is .0169 which is larger than our upper specification limit. This means a proportion of the lids will be too loose. To determine how many we go back to the number of standard deviations beyond the specification limit and the normal distribution table.

$$\frac{\text{Upper Spec Limit} - \overline{X}_c}{s} = \frac{(.015 - .0115)}{.0018} = 1.94 \text{ Standard Deviations}$$

At 1.94 σ from the mean, 2.62% of the area under the normal curve lies beyond that point so 2.62% of the lids will be loose.

In using statistical techniques, it begins to become apparent that it is no longer appropriate to use only numbers or absolute values in making judgements. The phenomena of variation means that you could have selected at random an object from the high side of process number one and the low side of process number two. A judgement that process number one was better could have been made causing the removal or closing of process number two.

The possibility that both were running with the same average and standard deviation and as such were identical would have remained untested.

The Chi Square Analysis

To test this possibility in a statistical context we have to compare our observed data with what we will call the expected data. The resulting **Chi square statistic** of that comparison is compared with a critical value to determine if the differences we are looking at are statistically significant.

This is accomplished in the following manner.

For each piece of data:
$$\frac{(O-E)^2}{E}$$

O = the observed number

E = the expected number

And the Chi squared statistic;

$$\Sigma \frac{(\text{observed number - expected number})^2}{\text{expected number}} \text{ or}$$

$$\Sigma \frac{(O - E)^2}{E}$$

In the following example we will use this to see if there is any real difference between how two people are doing their job even though the numbers seem to say there is.

We have two artists. Each of them completed two hundred jobs last month. The first artist had seven returns and the second had fifteen. What should we do?

Fraction nonconforming

Artist #1	7/200 =	.035
Artist #2	15/200 =	.075
Overall	7ı15/200+200 =	.055

If both artists had the same fraction nonconforming, an estimate of that fraction based on the above data is .055.

Then, in a sample of 200 jobs we could expect to find:
(.055)(200) = 11 nonconforming
and good jobs:
(1-.055)(200) = 189 conforming
so we set up a table of observed counts:

	Artist #1	Artist#2
Nonconforming	7	15
Conforming	193	185

and a table of expected counts

	Artist #1	Artist#2
Nonconforming	11	11
Conforming	189	189

To compare these results, we use the Chi Square statistic

$$\sum \frac{(O - E)^2}{E}$$

For the two artists:

$$\sum \frac{(O - E)^2}{E} =$$

$$\frac{(7 - 11)^2}{11} + \frac{(193 - 189)^2}{189} + \frac{(15 - 11)^2}{11} + \frac{(185 - 189)^2}{189}$$

$$= 1.4545 + .0847 + 1.4545 + .0847$$

$$= 3.0784$$

We next determine the degrees of freedom in the table where the degrees of freedom = df =(number of rows - 1)(number of colums - 1)

$$= (2 - 1)(2 - 1) = (1)(1) = 1$$

Then we look up the critical value from the following Chi Square table. With this case, we have one degree of freedom and assuming we want a 95% confidence level, we select 3.84 as the critical value.

$(1 - .95) = .05.$

To interpret the Chi Square / Critical value Relationship

Range of Chi Square Values

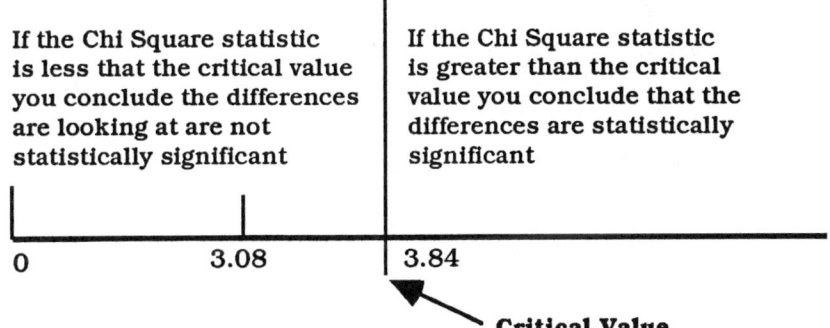

If the Chi Square statistic is less that the critical value you conclude the differences are looking at are not statistically significant

If the Chi Square statistic is greater than the critical value you conclude that the differences are statistically significant

0   3.08   3.84

Critical Value

The Chi Square statistic of 3.08 is less than 3.84 so we conclude that based upon the data thus far, there is no significant difference between the levels of performance of these two artists.

Chart Analysis

Critical Values of the Chi Square Distribution

df	.10	.05	.02	.01	.001
1	2.71	3.84	5.41	6.64	10.83
2	4.60	5.99	7.82	9.21	13.82
3	6.25	7.82	9.84	11.34	16.27
4	7.78	9.49	11.67	13.28	18.46
5	9.24	11.07	13.39	15.09	20.52
6	10.64	12.59	15.03	16.81	22.46
7	12.02	14.07	16.62	18.48	24.32
8	13.36	15.51	18.17	20.09	26.12
9	14.68	16.92	19.68	21.67	27.88
10	15.99	18.31	21.16	23.21	29.59
11	17.28	19.68	22.62	24.72	31.26
12	18.55	21.03	24.05	26.22	32.91
13	19.81	22.36	25.47	27.69	34.53
14	21.06	23.68	26.87	29.14	36.12
15	22.31	25.00	28.26	30.58	37.70
16	23.54	26.30	29.63	32.00	39.29
17	24.77	27.59	31.00	33.41	40.75
18	25.99	28.87	32.35	34.80	42.31
19	27.20	30.14	33.69	36.19	43.82
20	28.41	31.41	35.02	37.57	45.32
21	29.62	32.67	36.34	38.93	46.80
22	30.81	33.92	37.66	40.29	48.27
23	32.01	35.17	38.97	41.64	49.73
24	33.20	36.42	40.27	42.98	51.18
25	34.38	37.65	41.57	44.31	52.62
26	35.56	38.88	42.86	45.64	54.05
27	36.74	40.11	44.14	46.96	55.48
28	37.92	41.34	45,42	48.28	56.89
29	30.09	42.56	46.69	49.59	58.30
30	40.26	43.77	47.96	50.89	59.70

where α heads the columns.

Translating the Information

Comparing absenteeism rates among different departments is always interesting. In a study of employee absenteeism at one company it was decided to determine if all departments had about the same rate of absences. An absence was defined as one employee missing eight hours of work. Records in four departments over a period of four weeks revealed the following. These were five day workweeks.

| | Department | | | |
	A	B	C	D
Number of absences	60	32	27	37
Total number of employee days	1000	400	300	500

average absences = $\bar{P} = 156/2200 = .071$

Table of Observed

Absences	60	32	27	37
Present	940	368	273	463

Table of Expected

Absences	70.91	28.36	21.27	35.45
Present	929.09	371.64	278.73	464.55

$$\sum \frac{(O-E)^2}{E} = 4.0439 \qquad \text{Degrees of freedom} = (2-1)(4-1) = 3$$

The critical value at a 95% confidence level = 7.82

The conclusion therefore is there is no real difference among the absenteeism rates because 4.0439 is less than 7.82.

Comparing Different Operations

In applying ceramic decorations to coffee mugs an important quality characteristic for the decorator is the size consistency that exists from mug to mug. Too large a variation from the smallest to the largest mug can cause serious problems with the dimensional placement of the decoration as well as an inability to fit the mug on the printing machine or damage the equipment if the mug is too large.

This next example looks at the data gathered by a decorator who is attempting to compare the size variation from two factories supplying blank coffee mugs. One of the factories is in Indonesia, and the other is in China.

Factory:	**Indonesia**	**China**
sample size (n)	$n = 108$	$n = 40$
standard deviation	$s_i = .01146$	$s_c = .04085$
variance	$s_i^2 = .000131$	$s_c^2 = .001669$

To get the pooled estimate of common variance in measurements from two independent samples like these, we use the following.

$$S_p^{\,2} = \frac{(n_i - 1)(s_i^{\,2}) + (n_c - 1)(s_c^{\,2})}{n_i + n_c - 2}$$

We will be looking for a 95% confidence level in our statement about the difference between these two factories. This difference is expressed as;

$$\overline{X}_i' - \overline{X}_c'$$

$$(\overline{X}_i - \overline{X}_c) \pm ts_{\overline{X}_i - \overline{X}_c}$$

and

$$s_{\overline{X}_i - \overline{X}_c} = \sqrt{s_p^{\,2}\left(\frac{1}{n_i} + \frac{1}{n_c}\right)}$$

Table II on page 288 shows the value of t from the distribution table with $n_1 + n_2 - 2$ degrees of freedom corresponding to the confidence coefficient $1 - \alpha$ (95% in this case).

continuing;

$$\overline{X}_i - \overline{X}_c = 2.823 - 2.822 = .001$$

$$s_p^2 = \frac{(107)(.000131) + (39)(.001669)}{146}$$

$$= \frac{.0140 + .065}{146} = \frac{.079}{146} = .00054$$

$$s_{\bar{X}_i - \bar{X}_c} = \sqrt{(.00054)(\frac{1}{108} + \frac{1}{40}}$$

$$= \sqrt{(.00054)(.03425)} = \sqrt{.0000185} = .0043$$

For a confidence level of .95 and 146 degrees of freedom (df); $T = 1.98$

Confidence interval:
$$\bar{X} \pm ts = .001 \pm (1.98)(.0043)$$

$$= .001 \pm .008514 = -.0075; \ .009514$$

In this method of testing for signicant differences using the t test, we are looking for a confidence interval that covers the 0 value. Since this interval does cover 0, we conclude there is no real difference between the two plants with respect to the **average** sizes.

Now we know the average sizes of the mugs from the two plants are the same, we will check the differences in their part variation. This, after all, is the critical quality characteristic for the decorator.

To do this, we will use a different formula with a different table.

$$F_c = \frac{Larger\ s^2}{Smaller\ s^2}$$

$$= \frac{.001669}{.000131} = 12.7$$

This value is then compared to the critical value in Table II on page 288. If F_c is larger than the F_α value in the table, there is evidence of unequal variances in these two plants.

In using the table, the degrees of freedom for the numerator, which is the larger s^2, is determined by $V_1 = n - 1$. The denominator degrees of freedom is shown as $V_2 = n - 1$ for the smaller s^2.

In this table, 2α is the risk of concluding the two outputs have unequal variances when they do not.

In our case, our critical value given the degrees of freedom and confidence level is;

$$F_\alpha = 1.61 \qquad\qquad F_c = 12.7$$

With this difference we can conclude that the difference in size variance from these two plants is significantly different with the Indonesian plant producing with better quality characteristics.

Chart Analysis

Values of T
$(1 - \alpha)^*$

df	90	95	98	99
1	6.314	12.706	31.821	63.657
2	2.920	4.303	6.965	9.925
3	2.353	3.182	4.541	5.841
4	2.132	2.776	3.747	4.604
5	2.015	2.571	3.365	4.032
6	1.943	2.447	3.143	3.707
7	1.895	2.365	2.998	3.499
8	1.860	2.306	2.896	3.355
9	1.833	2.262	2.821	3.250
10	1.812	2.228	2.764	3.169
11	1.796	2.201	2.718	3.106
12	1.782	2.179	2.681	3.055
13	1.771	2.160	2.650	3.012
14	1.761	2.145	2.624	2.977
15	1.753	2.131	2.602	2.947
16	1.746	2.120	2.583	2.921
17	1.740	2.110	2.567	2.898
18	1.734	2.101	2.552	2.878
19	1.729	2.093	2.539	2.861
20	1.725	2.086	2.528	2.845
21	1.721	2.080	2.518	2.831
22	1.717	2.074	2.508	2.819
23	1.714	2.069	2.500	2.807
24	1.711	2.064	2.492	2.797
25	1.708	2.060	2.485	2.787
26	1.706	2.056	2.479	2.779
27	1.703	2.052	2.473	2.771
28	1.701	2.048	2.467	2.763
29	1.699	2.045	2.462	2.756
30	1.697	2.042	2.457	2.750
40	1.684	2.021	2.423	2.704
60	1.671	2.000	2.390	2.660
120	1.658	1.980	2.358	2.617
∞	1.645	1.960	2.326	2.576

* Area under T distribution curve over the interval from -T to +T for indicated degrees of freedom (df)

Adapted from Neter, Wasserman, and Whitmore, <u>Applied Statistics</u>, Allyn and Bacon, 1978.

Correlation and Regression

Correlation theory aids us in identifying relationships. If you ever wanted to know if something you were experiencing was caused or at least influenced by something else, this is the approach that will help you find an answer.

Are our observations interdependent? Does one affect the other, and if so, can we quantify the degree of that effect or the extent of the interdependence?

In one company, the percentage of on time delivery is thought to be related to the percentage of goods returned from the customer. The thought was expressed that perhaps questionable product was being shipped out rather than repaired or done over so it would show on time.

This observation may indicate a statistical association between the two variables of on time delivery, and customer returns.

We want to know what the degree of interdependence is and whether certain values of the two variables tend to occur together. Here is the data for the last ten months.

Chart Analysis

Y On Time Delivery	X Percentage Returns
86.9	1.02
89.9	1.11
90.3	1.43
87.3	1.11
92.6	1.01
87.3	.95
86.8	1.11
91.9	.87
95.6	1.43
89.9	1.02

Plotting the Data Vertically:

Percentage On Time Delivery Versus Percentage Returns

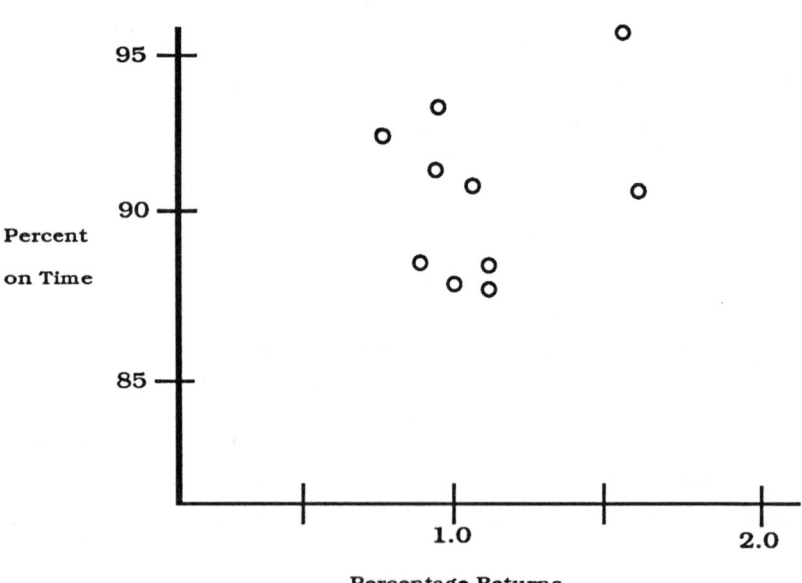

The following formula is used to determine the simple linear correlation coefficient.

$$R_{YX} = \frac{\sum X_i Y_i - N\overline{X}\,\overline{Y}}{(n-1)\,s_x s_y}$$

The first thing that stands out here is there is quite a bit of scatter when the data is plotted on a graph. This would be caused from other as yet unidentified variables besides X affecting Y and those variables were not held constant during this observation period.

There could also be some measurement error in the way we determined on time delivery and percentage returns.

A third reason could be that the real relationship is very complicated. When this happens, we will just approximate it.

To do this, we will use the r statistic.

In some relationships, the picture is very linear and easy to see. An example of a deterministic relationship like this would be the one between overtime and weekly pay.

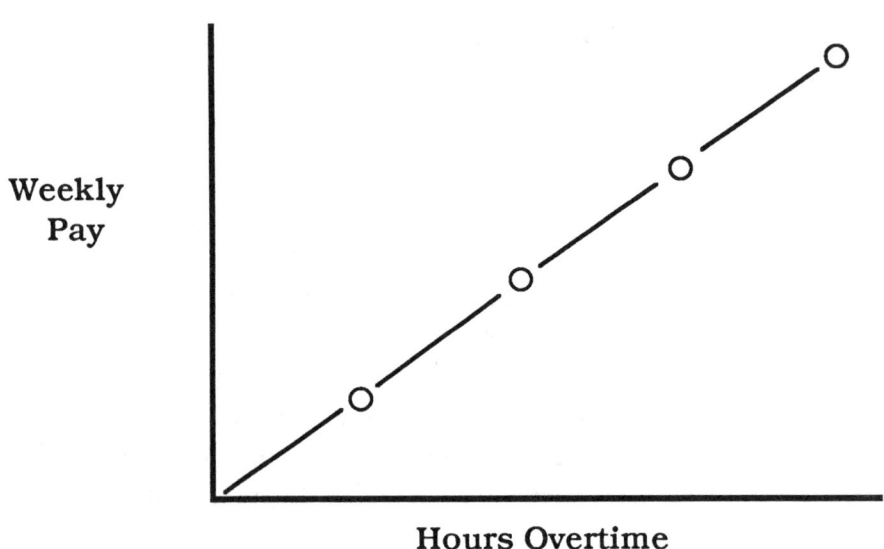

<u>Deterministic Relationship</u>

Weekly
Pay

Hours Overtime

Statistical relationships are not as clear.

Statistical relationship

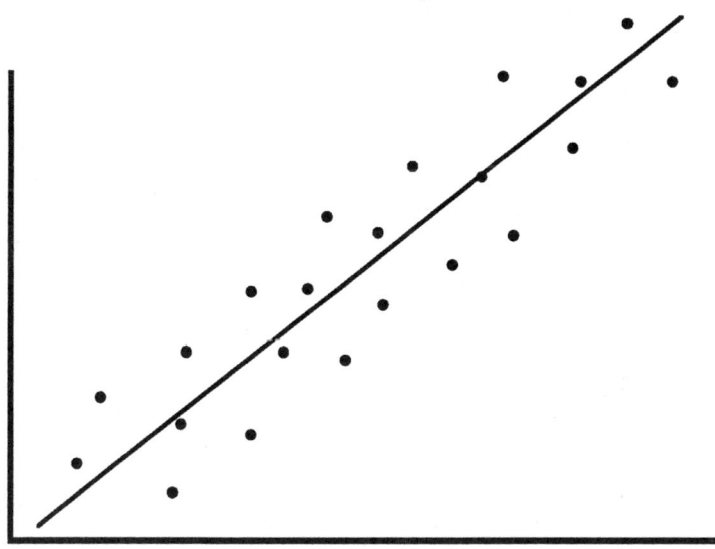

In a statistical relationship such as this, r is used to describe the interdependence.

Mathematically;

$$-1 \leq r \leq 1$$

The closer r is to either of the extremes, the stronger the relationship is.

For example:

For r = -1, the relationship is perfectly linear.

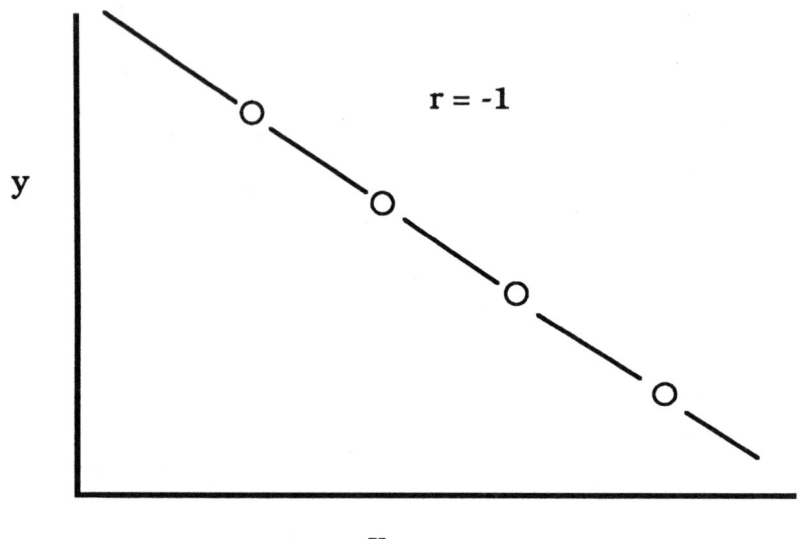

r = -1

y

x

For r = + 1, the relationship is also perfectly linear

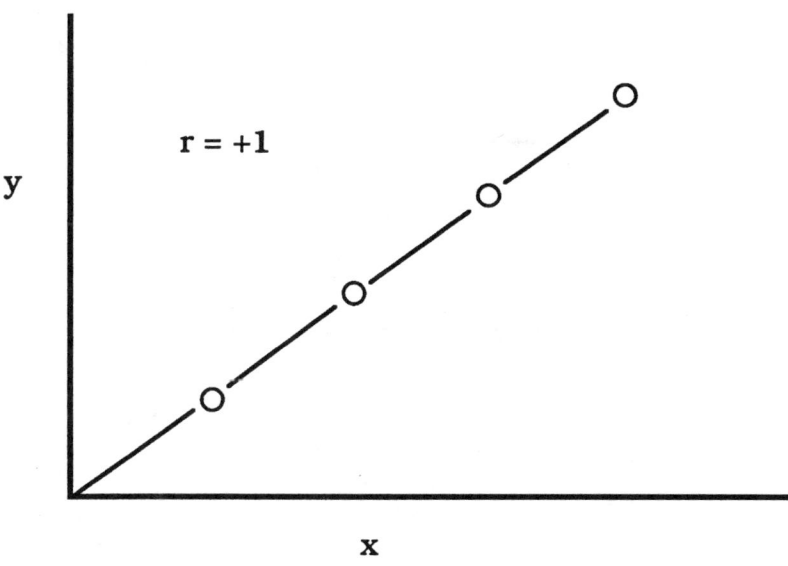

For r = 0, there is no slope so there is no linear correlation.

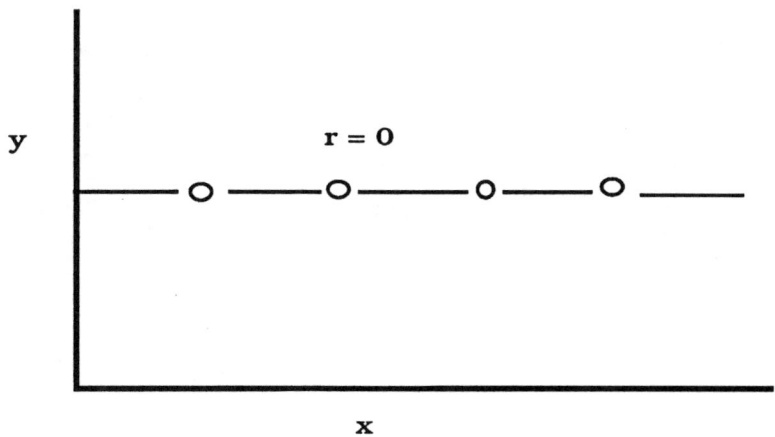

Chart Analysis

or

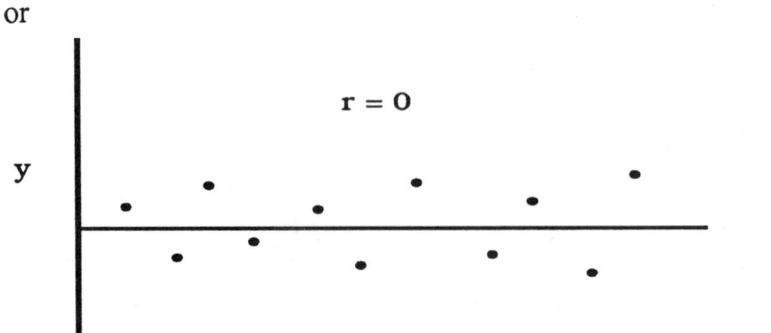

So in setting up the data for our problem we have;

Y	X	XY
86.9	1.02	88.638
89.9	1.11	99.789
90.3	1.43	129.129
86.3	1.11	95.793
92.6	1.01	93.526
87.3	.95	82.935
86.8	1.11	96.348
91.9	.87	79.953
95.6	1.43	136.708
89.9	1.02	<u>91.698</u>
		994.517

$$\bar{Y} = 89.75 \qquad s_y = 3.01929$$

$$\bar{X} = 1.106 \qquad s_x = .186798$$

$$\sum X_i Y_i \ = \ 994.517$$

$$\sum X_i Y_i - n\overline{X}\,\overline{Y} = (994.517) - [(10)(89.75)(1.106)]$$
$$= 994.517 - 992.635 = 1.882$$

$$(n-1)(s_X s_Y) \ = \ (9)(3.01929)(.186798) = 5.0760$$

$$R_{YX} \ = \ \frac{1.882}{5.0760} \ = \ .3708$$

The formula used to indicate the proportion of the observed variation that is linearly associated with changes in the process variable is;

$$(100)R_{YX}^{\,2}$$

With one on time delivery variable and one percentage returns variable this case has one degree of freedom in the numerator and (n - 2) degrees of freedom in the denominator for an F test.

If $\dfrac{R_{YX}^{\,2}}{1-R_{YX}^{\,2}}(n-2)$ exceeds the critical value from an F table, the relationship is said to be statistically significant.

For our case with n = 10 and R_{YX} = .3708;

$$(100)R_{YX}^{\,2} = (100)(.3708)^{2} = 13.75\%$$

Chart Analysis

$$F = \frac{(.3708)^2}{1-(.3708)^2}(10-2) \;=\; 1.28$$

And is less than the critical value of 7.57 for one degree of freedom in the numerator and 8 degrees of freedom in the denominator. This indicates this relationship is not statistically interdependent.

Sometimes it is simpler and faster to get an idea of the magnitude of r and the degree of interdependence just by looking at a graph of the information plotted on a X;Y graph.

Here is a picture of the correlation between values of r and the amount of scatter on one of these graphs.

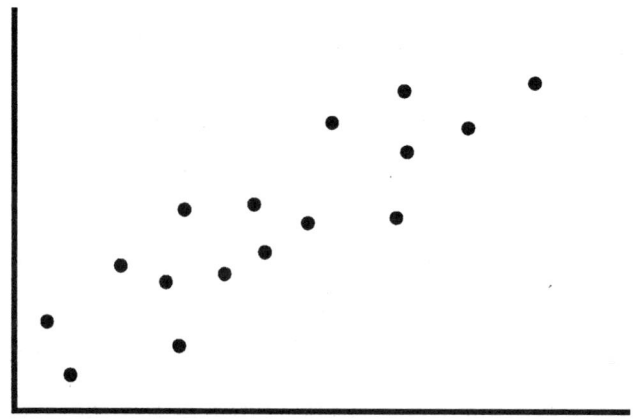

r = .9

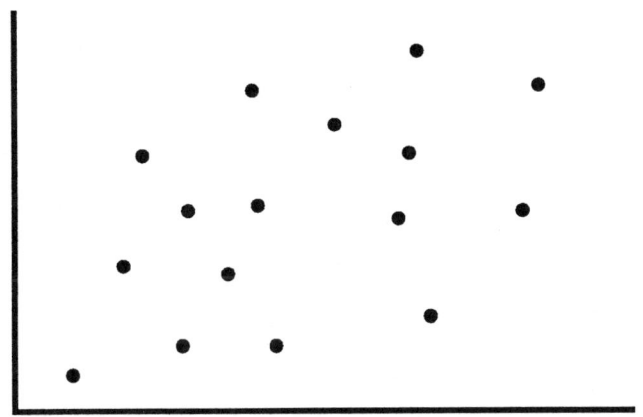

r = .5

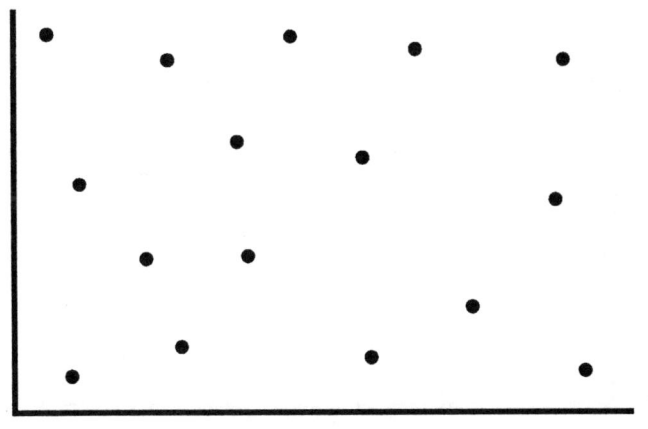

r = 0

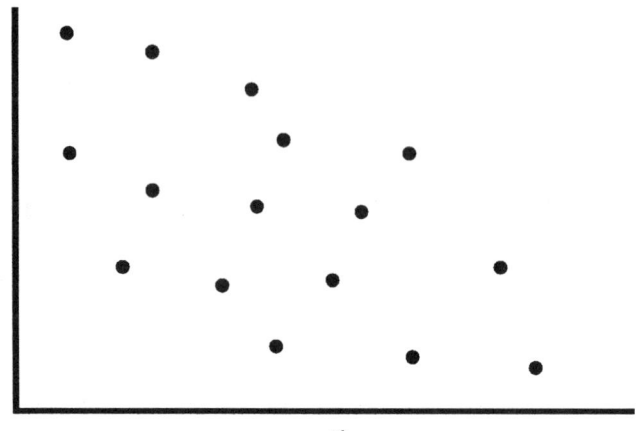

r = -.5

r = -.9

So far, we have been using r in measuring the extent of linear correlation. Here are some examples of sample results which would indicate no linear association.

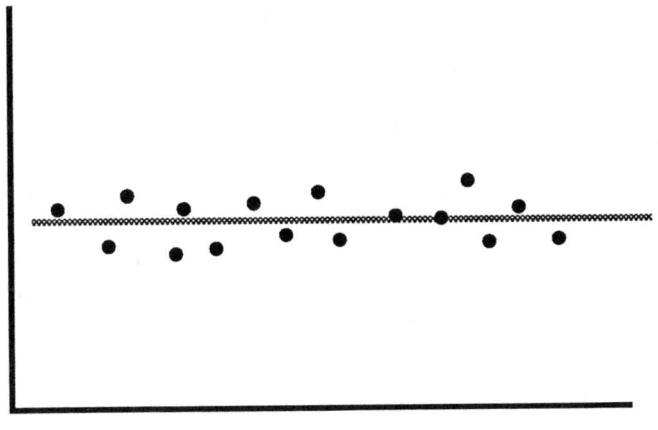

r = 0

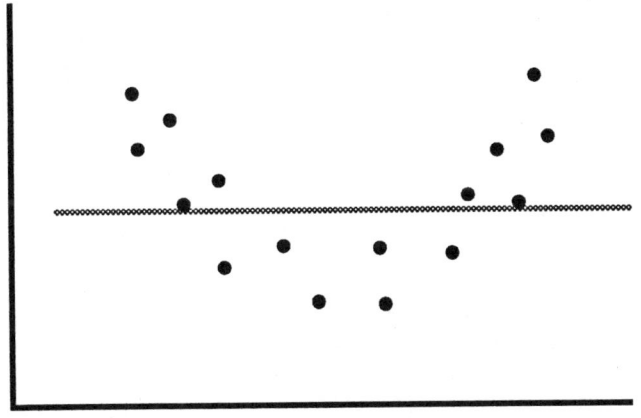

r = 0

Chart Analysis

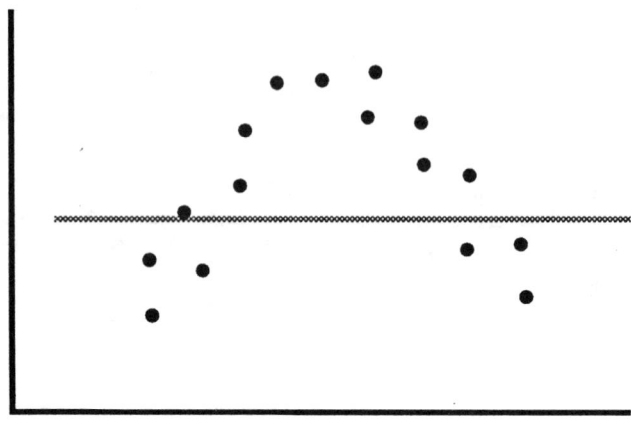

r = 0

The Visual Factory

If you plan for a year, plant a seed.
If for ten years, plant a tree.
If for a hundred years, teach the people.
When you sow a seed once, you will reap a single harvest.
When you teach the people, you will reap a hundred harvests.

Kuan Chung

Though Peter Drucker is often credited with coining the phrase "Management by Objectives", he is seldom remembered for the complete concept he was referring to and that is Management by Objectives **and self control.** Self control is the most powerful level of control and it is the driving principle behind the visual factory.

Self control means stronger motivation. It's a desire to be the best rather than just good enough to get by. Control is an ambiguous word that implies the ability to direct one's self and one's work. It can also describe a situation where one person can dominate another.

The visual factory enables us to substitute management by self control for management by domination. With self control, people are controlling themselves all the time. When the control comes from a dominating person, the situation is under good control only when that person is around.

An Abundance of Measurements

To be able to control their performance, groups of people need to know more than just what their goals are. They have to be able to measure performance and results against the goal. There should be an abundance of simple, clear, and common measurements in all key areas of an organization.

These measurements do not have to be rigidly quantitative nor do they need to be precise. They have to be simple, clear, relevant, and they should direct attention to where any efforts should go. They have to be able to speak for themselves in a self explanatory understandable way that does not require philosophical discussion or complicated interpretation.

Each department should have the information they need to measure their own performance and they should receive it early enough so they can make any changes necessary to get the desired results. This information should go directly to the department itself and not to management.

It should be a means for self control and not control from above. Managers who are genuinely interested will go to the departments themselves to get this information and see how things are going.

The visual factory assumes that people want to be responsible, want to contribute, want to achieve, and even today that is a bold set of assumptions to make for some yet we all know that people act largely as they are expected to act.

A management that starts out with the assumption that people are weak, irresponsible, and lazy will get weakness,

254

irresponsibility, and laziness. There is a self fulfilling prophecy here and that management will corrupt its own organization.

A management that assumes strength, responsibility, and a desire to contribute will experience some disappointments, but since the task at hand is to develop the strengths of the people, and because this can only be done by starting out with the assumption that people want to achieve, this is a necessary phase.

The Principles of Self Control

For years Management by Objectives has been a widely used slogan. There is a whole literature and any number of seminars and management courses on the subject. Literally thousands of companies have adopted a version of the policy of management by objectives but only a few have followed through with true self control.

By tying in the following principles of a visual factory with a broad charting program you have the basis for comprehensive feedback and a company run under the principles of self control.

To begin with, how would you describe your workplace? Does it fit with your vision of how it should be? How would you describe it visually in terms of being able to understand what is going on? Is all the information you need available and displayed? Can you look at it at a glance and understand how things are going?

What information that you are not getting do you need to have things run more smoothly? These questions are designed to stimulate a visual workplace vision. Such a vision is as follows.

The Visual Workplace

1. There is a place for everything and everything is in its place.

2. Storage areas are clearly marked and there is nothing unneeded outside those clearly marked areas.

3. There are marked and separate containers for scrap, rework, trash etc.

4. The place is clean from wall to wall.

5. Quality information, schedules, and processes are recognizable at a glance.

6. Waste and other problems are immediately apparent to everyone.

7. The work flow and everything else that is happening in the factory is readily apparent at a glance.

8. Standard procedures and operations descriptions are easily understood and visually clear.

Activities That do not Add Value

When you really look at a process, it is not uncommon to find that up to ninety five percent of the activity you observe is not adding value to your end product. A visual factory is set up so that all this non value added activity really stands out so it can be seen and addressed. Some examples of areas to be focused on with visual measurements and controls are:

- Material handling and transportation - though necessary, any at all is really too much.
- Storage or inventory
- Defects
  - -Raw material
  - - in process
  - - poor finished product quality
  - - spoilage
- Waiting
- Rework and inspection
- Overproduction
- Equipment downtime

Zero level targeting in eight key areas can provide a rallying point for performance measurements and improvement activities.

1. Zero waste   lower costs and capacity to do more

2. Zero defects   same

3. Zero accidents   improved safety

4. Zero downtime   better maintenance

5. Zero delays   reliable suppliers

6. Zero set up time   more diversified products

7. Zero customer complaints   seen as reliable supplier

8. Zero inventory   lower costs

Areas for Visual Controls

There are six areas that form the foundation for effective visual controls. They are:

- Orderliness
- Safety
- Organization
- Cleanliness
- Neatness
- Discipline

To be **orderly** means to set things in order, set limits, and share information. Determine the type of storage and layout for everything that is needed that guarantees the required amounts of the necessary items will be in their place when needed.

Make each space and location self explanatory so that everyone knows what goes where; and self regulatory using height and size limits such as marking the maximum height of storage to control the amount of material that is in there.

Also, set limits on item usage. Make sure established limits are adhered to by using, for example, standard container pallets that automatically control the quantity moved, held, or used.

The following photographs are from a factory that was transformed simply by marking off some areas on the floor with tape and using some identifying signs.

This first picture shows the assembly department before the visual markings were laid out.

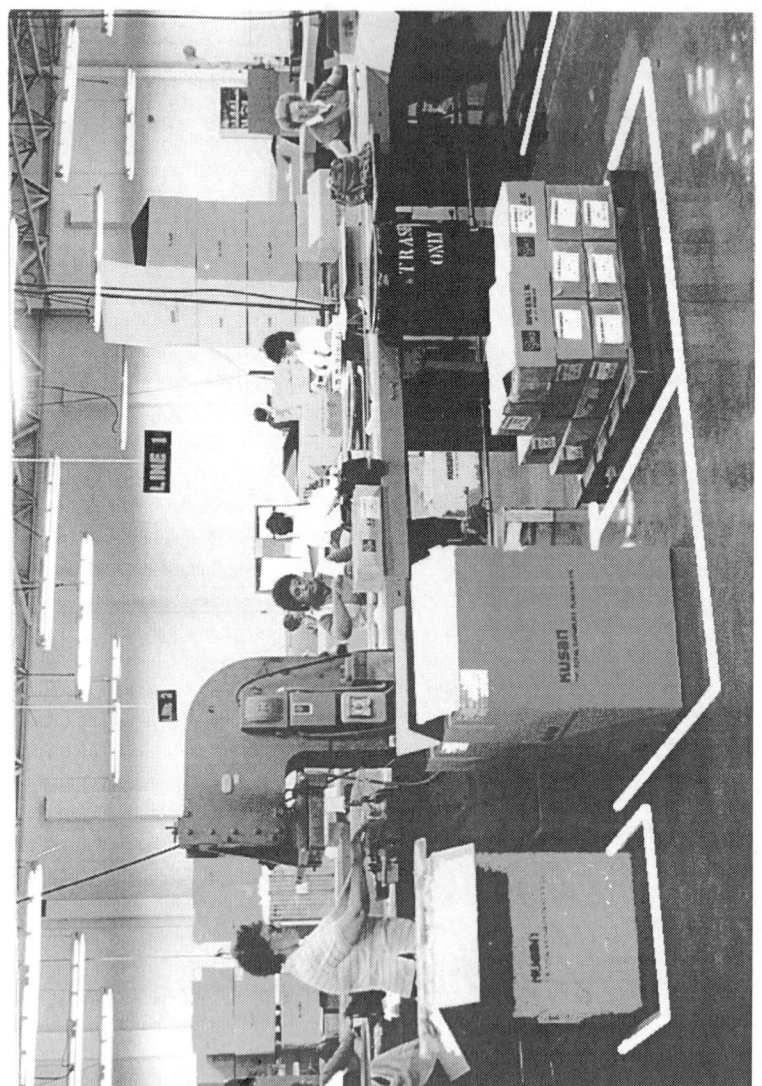

This is what the same department looked like after the addition of some floor taping and simple visual identification.

Organization means to sort through and sort out. Make clear distinctions between what is needed and what is not needed. Spot paint, red tag, or use other techniques to identify, separate, and dispose of unneeded items. Find out of the way storage for tools, parts and items that are not used daily. After you do this, outline procedures and measures to prevent the re accumulation of unnecessary items.

Shine everything, the equipment, the tools, the whole workplace. Keep the workplace swept up, wiped down, and clean. Eliminate dirt, dust, oil, scrap, and other foreign matter to make the workplace clean. Establish cleaning as a form of inspection. Cleaning exposes abnormalities and helps to identify normal and abnormal conditions. This allows corrections prior to failure in many cases. Integrate cleaning into everyday maintenance tasks. Investing personal time in cleaning and maintenance builds value for the equipment and pride in the work area.

Maintaining the Vision

When the workplace has been organized, made orderly, and cleaned up, a state of neatness has been reached. This state is maintained by;

- Sharing information so there is no searching.
- Standardizing everything so that all abnormalities can be easily and immediately recognized.

Information such as delivery dates, quality, attendance, downtime, etc., must be easily and visually available. Standards for procedures, quantities, and quality must be so clear and visible that abnormalities can be seen at a glance when they occur.

This can become a permanent state when ways are devised to prevent abnormalities from occurring. In order to do this, good root cause analysis has to be practiced to identify the source of errors or deviations from standards.

Discipline in this context means shaping the behavior of the group, not the elimination of organizational sin. You want people to be able to think and act on their feet and to adapt quickly to changing conditions. In the technical area you want things done by the book. In these areas, make a steady habit of properly maintaining correct procedures. Achieving the discipline of complete adherence to correct procedures depends on training and management.

Training is necessary to change work habits so the behavior in the work place is guided by a set of basic fundamental rules. A well ordered technical workplace runs by the book.

Take this checklist, and using it evaluate your workplace using very high standards. The more problem areas you find, the more opportunities for organizational improvement.

Visual Factory Inspection Sheet	Score	1: Perfect 2: Problems 3: Poor	Dept A	Dept B	Dept C	Dept D
Category	**Item**					
Orderliness	Is Everything in its own marked place?					
	Are the work areas clear and uncluttered?					
	Is everything put away after use?					
Safety	Are the Safety boards posted and up to date?					
	Are the unsafe act ID cards complete and current?					
Organization	Are aisles and work areas clearly outlined?					
	Is the information posted on the boards neatly?					
	Is it clear why any unusual items are present?					
	Have all unnecessary items been removed?					
Cleanliness	Is the machinery and equipment clean?					
	Are the work areas clean?					
	Are the marking lines clean and unbroken?					
Neatness	Is the area free of trash and debris?					
	Are cleanup responsibilities assigned?					
	Has the floor been cleaned?					
	Have all the machines and work areas been cleaned?					
Discipline	Are private belongings put away?					
	Is there no eating or drinking in the workplace?					
	Are the smoking areas observed?					
	Are private conversations avoided during worktime?					

Total ◯◯◯◯

Visual control is the type of control that enables any person, even those who know very little about the specific work place, to recognize at a glance standards and necessary information

263

as well as any problems, abnormalities, waste, or deviations from standards.

Get the correct information or standard as closely to the point of action as possible. Ideally, integrate the standard totally with the action.

A System of Visual Controls

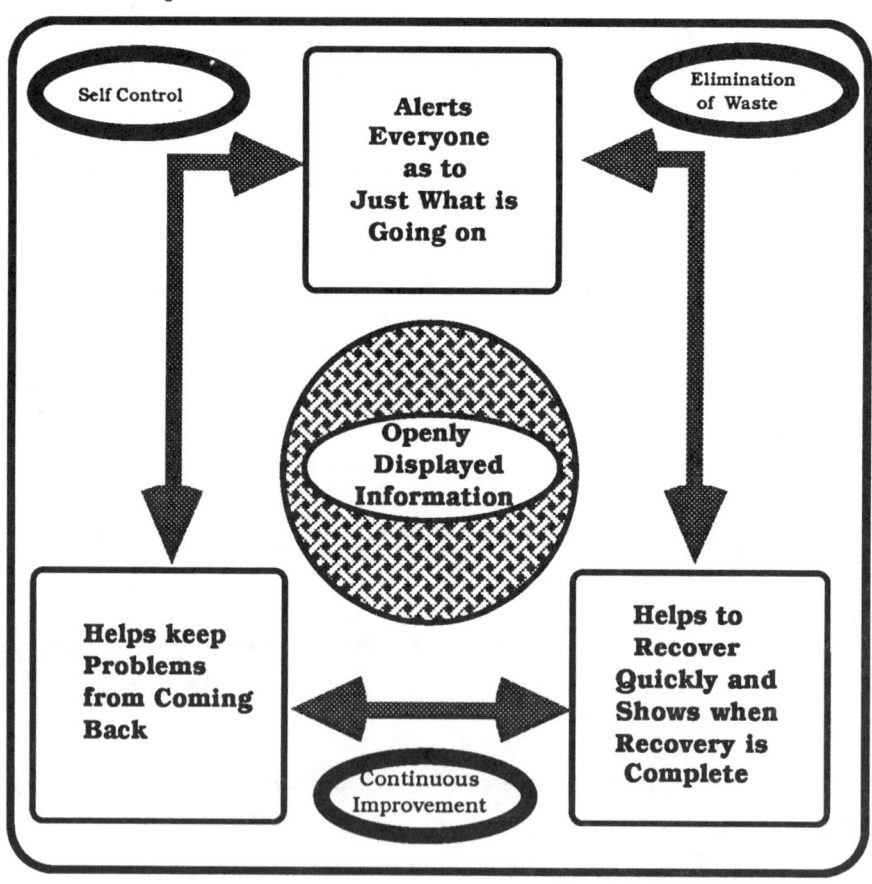

There is a seven step process in building this visual factory.

1. Determine the information that will be needed to control the shop and improve the processes.

2. Share this information and the results of the control activities by displaying on prominent boards throughout the company.

3. Standardize as much as possible and communicate these standards.

4. Build these standards into the workplace.

5. Build in alarms that will show the abnormalities when compared with these standards.

6. Prevent any defects from moving on through the system.

7. Mistake - proof (Poka Yoke) the process to prevent abnormalities.

Red Lined work areas.

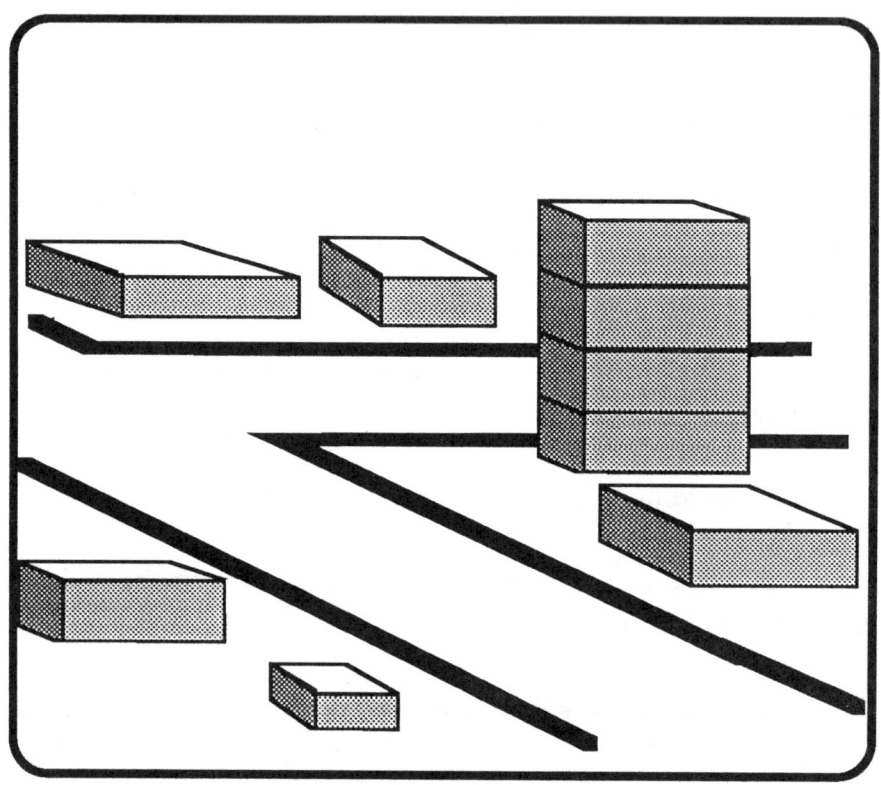

When organizing the shop floor in an orderly fashion, mark out all aisle ways with red tape to also indicate exit routes. Storage areas may be marked with yellow tape . If you are certain these designations will ***never*** change they can be painted on the floor. Using tape allows flexibility for change in the future without having confusing older lines painted on the floor.

Red Line Indicators

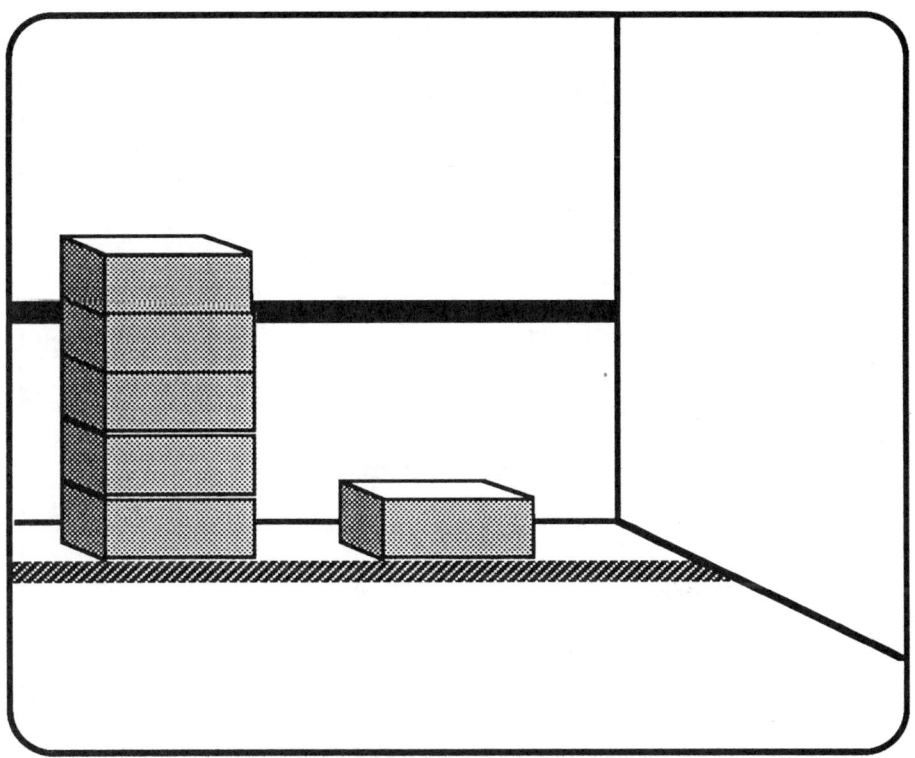

    The line taped on the wall becomes part of the visual strategy. Anything stacked up higher than the line shows excess inventory.

Department Signboards

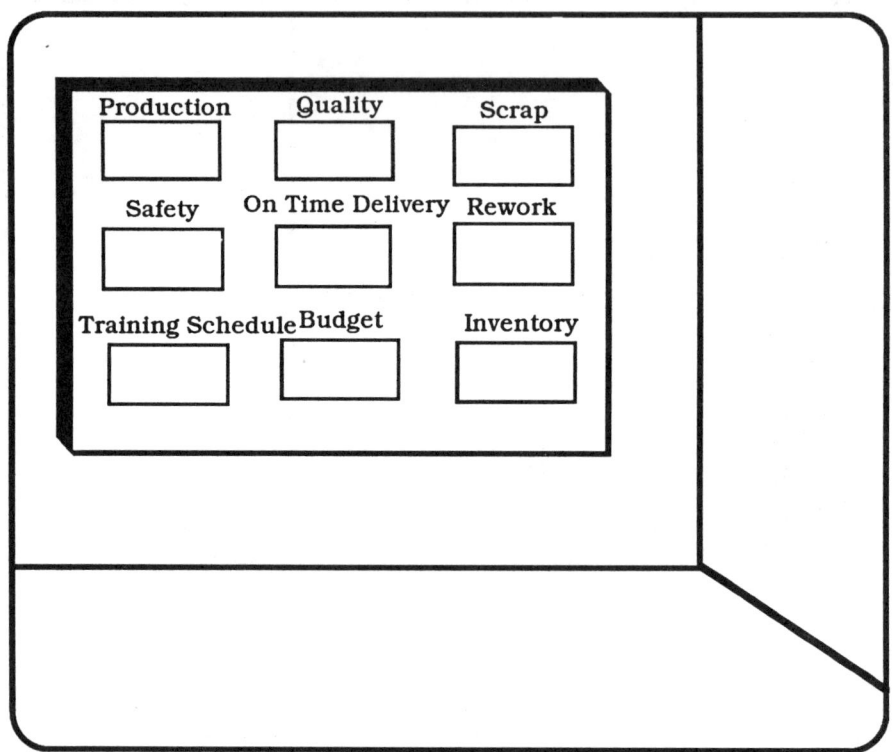

These are display boards that include charted information on anything you are measuring.

Red Tags

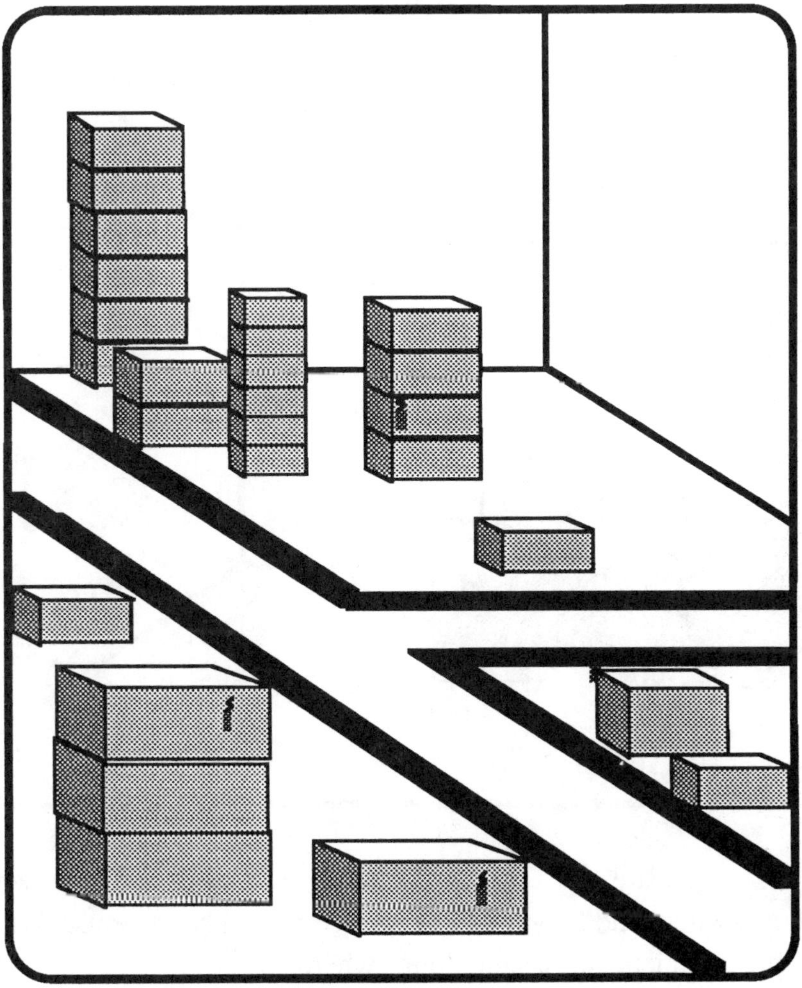

Using red tags helps distinguish between needed and unneeded items on the shop floor. Red tags mark the items that are to be removed.

Identifying Signs

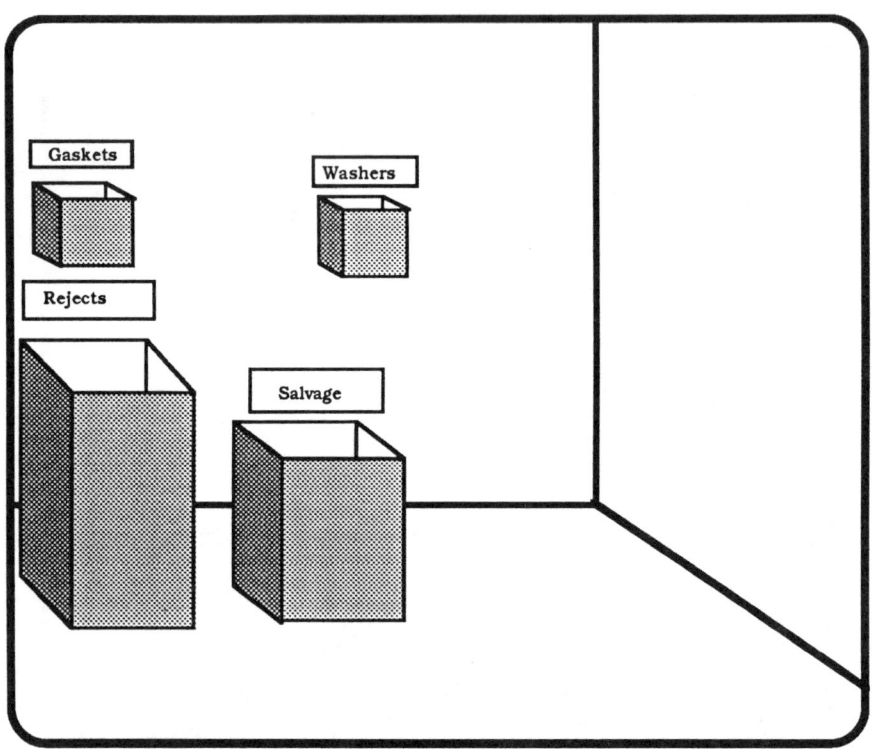

Signs are set up over all storage bins to indicate what belongs where and how much of it there should be. Anyone should be able to understand what belongs where.

Alarm Lights

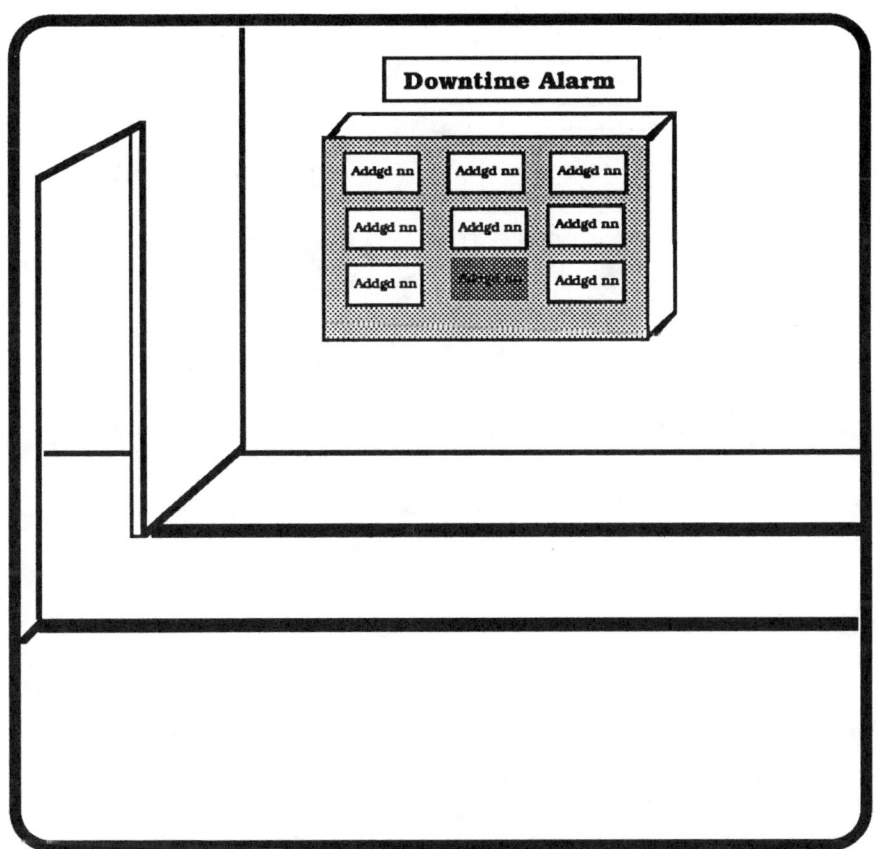

Downtime alarm lamps immediately alert people to abnormalities in the plant as soon as they enter the shop floor. These signals can also be located throughout the plant.

Defective Item Displays

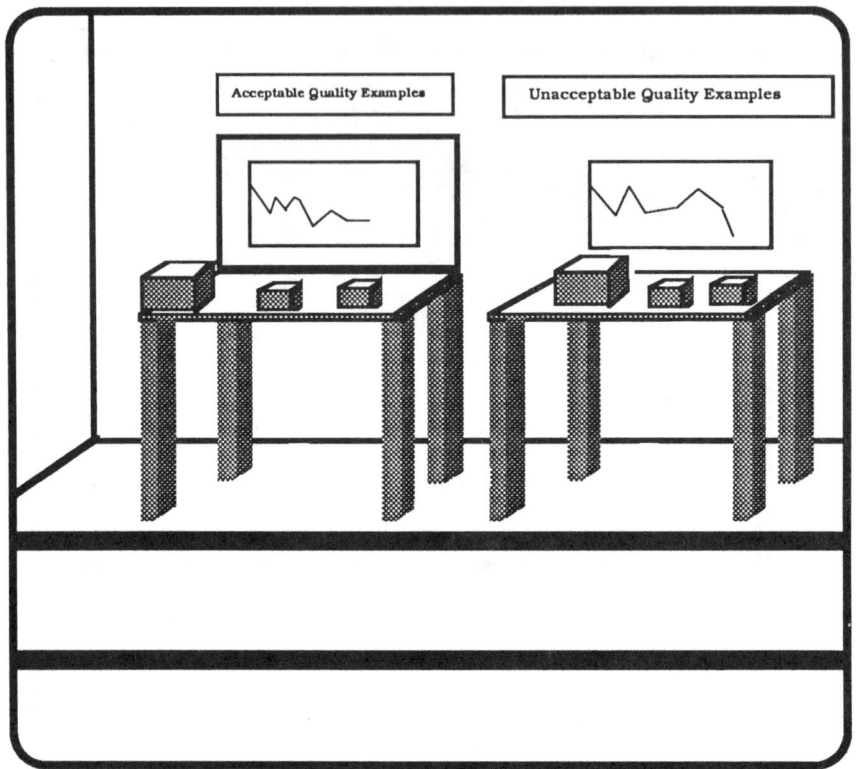

These displays are set up throughout the shop. They have examples of acceptable and unacceptable quality as well as graphic representation of what is happening to those quality levels.

Keys to Success in Organizing the Workplace

After a big initial push to achieve some of the steps indicated so far, you may have succeeded in getting rid of unnecessary items, marked off areas for storing things, and cleaned everything in the shop from wall to wall.

All this means nothing unless there is also established a system for maintaining all of these improvements.

The following are a few points that can serve as keys to success in establishing and maintaining a visual workplace.

- Get everyone involved
- The final responsibility rests with the Top Manager who should inspect the factory personally.
- Make everything understood.
- Do it all the way. No half hearted efforts here
- Don't stop halfway
- These improvements are a bridge to further improvements.

Reasons for Implementation Failures

Here are some reasons for the inadequate implementation of a visual factory.

The Visual Factory

• Leaping into immediate remedial measures without understanding the main purpose of visual controls is to first make any waste or abnormality in the workplace visible to the eye.

• A low level of problem consciousness among all employees

• Inadequate visual control resulting in their lack of use and no real control.

• Inadequate training in the use of the visual controls.

• No involvement in visual controls from non - manufacturing employees.

• Visual controls were put in before any mechanisms were established for the smooth performance of the work.

Communicating Diversity of Knowledge

An important measure in establishing a flow system is the level of skill diversity among the employees. You need to know who can step up and pitch in if a key group member is missing or otherwise engaged. A visual display such as the following has been used by many to show the extent of this skill diversity.

Skill Diversity   Cutting Department

Personnel	Operations										
	1	**2**	**3**	**4**	**5**	**6**	**7**	**8**	**9**	**10**	**11**
AA	Learning				Learning					Learning	
Bb		Mastered Repetitive		Can Teach			Can Teach			Mastered Repetitive	
Cc	Learning		Learning			Mastered Repetitive					
Dd		Mastered Repetitive	Mastered Repetitive		Mastered Rep. & QC						
Ee									Mastered Rep. & QC		
Ff				Learning						Can Teach	
Gg			Mastered Rep. & QC			Learning		Learning			
Hh	Mastered Repetitive							Can Teach			
Ii		Learning								Mastered Repetitive	
Jj			Can Teach		Learning		Mastered Repetitive				
Kk						Mastered Repetitive		Can Teach			
Ll	Mastered Rep. & QC		Learning						Learning		

■ = Learning   ■■ / ■ = Mastered Repetitive Functions and Quality Control

■■ = Mastered Repetitive Functions   ■■/■■ = Can Teach

The Customer Feedback Loop

Just as feedback from controlling activities improves the planning process, feedback from customers can improve the process of providing customer satisfaction. There are many different means to accomplish this but what will be reviewed here are some actual examples that are practical and have worked in the field.

First of all, anyone who has contact with customers should be solicited for feedback often and completely. A good source is the sales force itself. A practice that should be initiated immediately if it is not already in effect is the sales call report.

This is a simple report along the lines of the suggested format below. It should be completed daily and submitted weekly. This report provides the means to:

- Track the activity of the sales force.

- Build a customer contact history file.

- Obtain feedback from the customer.

- Help plan the activities of the sales force.

Customer; Date, Contact, Address	Products Reviewed and Comments
	Favorable;
	Unfavorable
	The Competition
	Favorable;
	Unfavorable
	The Competition
	Favorable;
	Unfavorable
	The Competition
	Favorable;
	Unfavorable
	The Competition

If this report is filled out promptly while the information is still fresh, you can get the beginnings of a continuous history of what your customers are saying about you.

Communicating the News

If the reports are submitted in a timely manner this information can be quickly distributed to other areas of the company. As each area manager gets an update, a simple highlighting of the comments applying to that area and posting a copy of the highlighted report on a separate "Our Customers Comment About Us" information board provides fresh and timely feedback to those in a position to act on the customer concerns.

This won't do it all in terms of letting you find out what your customers think of you, but it is a beginning.

There could be problems if this were the only type of feedback relied upon in that there is the possibility for editorial and even censorship work on the part of those writing the report.

Direct, regular copies distributed throughout the company regularly are an excellent vehicle to stir people into action to deal with a dissatisfied customer, however, phone calls are also important. Why are they calling? How often are they calling? Who are they calling? If you have a great deal of phone contact with your customers you are losing a good opportunity to get feedback if you do not organize this information on a daily basis and distribute it weekly.

Rather than just record how many calls are coming in, have the telephone correspondents use a Pareto type checklist. They list seven common reasons for a call plus "other". If "other" gets too popular, trade it for the least indicated of the seven main categories. Not only does this give a good visual picture of this form of customer contact, any shift in customer concerns can be detected and displayed right away.

Fast resolution of a problem begins with the fast recognition of a problem.

Again, all of this information should be posted on a very visual "Why are our customers calling us?" information board. The efforts at feedback are to improve service so if something can be done to the process to eliminate or greatly reduce the number one reason they are calling us, we have improved service.

Another type of checklist is to record where the calls are coming from. Is there an area of the country or sales territory that is not getting enough sales attention so the customers have to call in for help? Is there an area of unusually high call rates signaling perhaps more economic activity in that area? How about an area with a significantly lower call rate?   If you had this type of feedback you would have more information as to where to direct your sales activity.

What you need to have is a historical record of this calling activity. This allows you to get right to the meat of the problem whenever negative customer feedback is a problem, and around a lot of emotional guesswork as to just what might be the real problem.

You also need to have a record of why you are calling them. Who are you calling? Where? Why? How often? If things were going OK, most of these calls could probably be eliminated. The fact that we are making these calls and are not getting or using this type of information means we are losing an opportunity to improve service. How many outgoing calls are we making each day and for what reason? Use a Pareto type chart. Update it daily and closely monitor any shifts or trends.

Asking for Feedback

Telemarketing is an important tool in soliciting customer feedback. Though often associated with presenting a company to its customer base, a telemarketing approach to asking what the customers think is also effective. It usually comes in the form of a relatively short list of potential questions structured so the answer can be responded to simply and the data can be recorded and organized easily.

If the company sales are coming in slower than expected or a weakness is showing up in one of the product lines   you can sit and wonder what is going on or you can get on the phone and find out exactly from your customers.

When you do this, prepare well with a brief but thorough questionnaire. Don't use up more of your customer's time than necessary with a poorly organized set of questions.

If you have a long laundry list of areas you want feedback on, use a survey. This can be filled out and marked in at your customer's convenience. This format can provide you with a broader base of information than the telemarketing survey can provide and it doesn't ask your customer to lose much time off the job.

A version of the survey is the telephone survey system that allows your customers to respond to questions via a touch tone phone. There are companies who will customize a survey/ system to fit your company's needs. This system can greatly reduce the administrative hassles and data processing time.

It also doesn't have the time and cost involved with printing, distributing, mailing, and collecting surveys. Since the data is collected automatically, you are very quickly provided with accurate, easy to read, and graphical reports. It also allows you to survey your customers at their convenience and still get you the quick results you want.

Auditing How Customers are Treated

Much as in the same way you have an auditing firm to validate the financial performance of your company, you can do the same thing to audit how your customers are being treated. You can contract for an outside organization or individual to pose as a customer and unknown to your sales force, receptionist, customer service, credit, planning, and shipping people, evaluate their performance and provide you with feedback and trend reports on just how well they are treated in their encounters with your company.

Shop your company. Take some of that money you have set aside for market research and buy some of your own products. Become a customer. At the same time you enter orders for your own company buy the same items from your best competitor. Build up a good first hand information base that compares you with others in terms of:

- Lead Times
- Frequency, type, and quality of customer service interactions.
- Access to order information while it is being produced.
- Quality of communications when problems arise.
- On time delivery performance.
- Product quality
- Warranty and claims follow-up service.

Pick out other areas that are of concern to you and measure them as well. Do this on a regular basis and analyze any trends that exist. Which way is your performance relative to your competition going? What are their strengths? . . . . Weaknesses? How about yours?

Without tipping your hand, share the results of this information with everyone concerned. They need to know. Do it in a way that gets them this information without allowing them to determine how to know when they are working on your orders.

They have to believe they are working on just a average customer so they will provide the typical service and you can evaluate just how effective that typical service is.

Trade Shows

If you go to a trade show, go prepared. This is your best opportunity as a manager to get feedback direct from the customer. Don't let them get away with anything on their mind.

Every company prepares those going to a trade show on how to promote the company and put its best foot forward. A lot of their efforts will be in promoting to those who are not already customers. They will also be dealing with current customers. Other than in providing information on what is new, the best use of this time with those customers is to find out how things are going.

Since no-one likes to deal with bad news, there is a tendency here to want to quickly move onto another subject or customer if a problem comes up. They want to minimize or move from the problem because it is painful to talk about it. In doing this, you are moving off an opportunity into safe territory.

Getting your money's worth from the cost of the show means you must get good customer feedback to tell you the issues you face and point you in the right direction. People have to be prepared to do this because it is not something they like to do naturally. Asking questions like "How are we doing?" are not going to cut it here.

A better question would be along the lines of "What would you like us to change in the way we do business with you?" Record the answers. Tabulate the answers. Use checklists if there are a lot of contacts with similar responses. Get the information down. Don't let it get away. It's the very starting point of making you a better supplier and in course a better company.

Communicate what you find out when the trade show is over. Post all the comments. Distribute a newsletter. Give yourself a score based on what you heard and compare it with scores you recorded in the past. What are the trends? Let this information become a rallying point for improvements you intend to make in the future.

The "Secret" Customer

Arrange with a "secret" customer to provide top management feedback. This should be an average size customer which could not expect any special treatment due to the volume of business they do. It seems that everyone is aware now that their largest customers have to be treated specially and for the most part, all appear to be doing a good job at that. We are going to be interested in seeing how the average or small customer is being treated.

The next breakthrough in good service will come from those who learn to provide exceptional service to the average and small customer. This holds true for just about any business.

You solicit the same type of information as in the other methods and you continuously track how you are doing. Use trend information and not absolute values to measure performance. Movies can tell more than snapshots. Post the results conspicuously so everyone can see how you are doing.

There may be the need for a time delay between the occurrence of events and the posting of feedback so as to maintain the confidentiality of who this secret customer is. Pretty soon people will be able to tie in this feedback with recent events and ascertain just who this secret customer is. If that happens and your secret customer begins to get special treatment unbeknownst to you, a very loud and false signal will be sent through your management system

That signal would be that even your average customers are now getting exemplary service.

If you begin shifting to an EDI format, do not let the efficiency of this communication format allow you to lose contact with your customer. Set up a message box or bulletin board to allow for the EDI of customer comments that can be printed out and posted on a regular basis. Encourage your customers to use this mechanism so they don't drift out of contact,

Now that you have all this feedback coming in you have to close the loop. This is the information that is going to help sharpen your planning process and it has to be handled well in order for this to happen.

Appendix

Table I

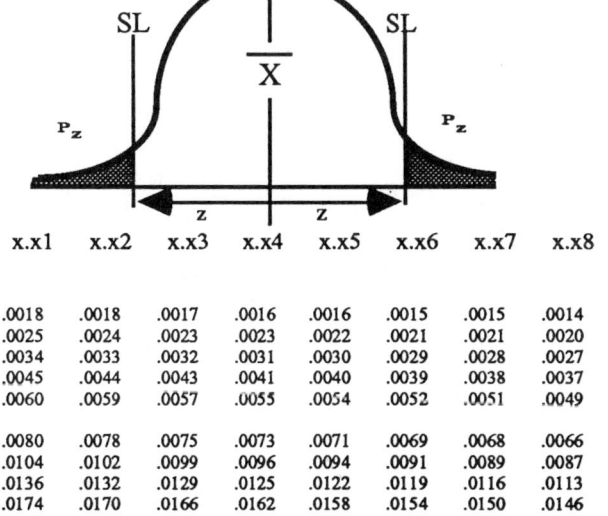

|z|	x.x0	x.x1	x.x2	x.x3	x.x4	x.x5	x.x6	x.x7	x.x8	x.x9
3.0	.00135									
2.9	.0019	.0018	.0018	.0017	.0016	.0016	.0015	.0015	.0014	.0014
2.8	.0026	.0025	.0024	.0023	.0023	.0022	.0021	.0021	.0020	.0019
2.7	.0035	.0034	.0033	.0032	.0031	.0030	.0029	.0028	.0027	.0026
2.6	.0047	.0045	.0044	.0043	.0041	.0040	.0039	.0038	.0037	.0036
2.5	.0062	.0060	.0059	.0057	.0055	.0054	.0052	.0051	.0049	.0048
2.4	.0082	.0080	.0078	.0075	.0073	.0071	.0069	.0068	.0066	.0064
2.3	.0107	.0104	.0102	.0099	.0096	.0094	.0091	.0089	.0087	.0084
2.2	.0139	.0136	.0132	.0129	.0125	.0122	.0119	.0116	.0113	.0110
2.1	.0179	.0174	.0170	.0166	.0162	.0158	.0154	.0150	.0146	.0143
2.0	.0228	.0222	.0217	.0212	.0207	.0202	.0197	.0192	.0188	.0183
1.9	.0287	.0281	.0274	.0268	.0262	.0256	.0250	.0244	.0239	.0233
1.8	.0359	.0351	.0344	.0336	.0329	.0322	.0314	.0307	.0301	.0294
1.7	.0446	.0436	.0427	.0418	.0409	.0401	.0392	.0384	.0375	.0367
1.6	.0548	.0537	.0526	.0516	.0505	.0495	.0485	.0475	.0465	.0455
1.5	.0668	.0655	.0643	.0630	.0618	.0606	.0594	.0582	.0571	.0559
1.4	.0808	.0793	.0778	.0764	.0749	.0735	.0721	.0708	.0694	.0681
1.3	.0968	.0951	.0934	.0918	.0901	.0885	.0869	.0853	.0838	.0823
1.2	.1151	.1131	.1112	.1093	.1075	.1056	.1038	.1020	.1003	.0985
1.1	.1356	.1335	.1314	.1292	.1271	.1251	.1230	.1210	.1190	.1170
1.0	.1587	.1562	.1539	.1515	.1492	.1469	.1446	.1423	.1401	.1379
0.9	.1884	.1814	.1788	.1762	.1736	.1711	.1685	.1660	.1635	.1611
0.8	.2119	.2090	.2061	.2033	.2005	.1977	.1949	.1922	.1894	.1867
0.7	.2420	.2389	.2358	.2327	.2297	.2266	.2236	.2206	.2177	.2148
0.6	.2743	.2709	.2676	.2643	.2611	.2578	.2546	.2514	.2483	.2451
.05	.3085	.3030	.3015	.2981	.2946	.2912	.2877	.2843	.2810	.2776
0.4	.3446	.3409	.3372	.3336	.3300	.3264	.3228	.3192	.3156	.3121
0.3	.3821	.3783	.3745	.3707	.3669	.3632	.3594	.3557	.3520	.3483
0.2	.4207	.4168	.4129	.4090	.4052	.4013	.3974	.3036	.3897	.3859
0.1	.4602	.4562	.4522	.4483	.4443	.4404	.4364	.4325	.4286	.4247
0.0	.5000	.4960	.4920	.4880	.4840	.4801	.4761	.4721	.4681	.4641

Table II

F_α For $\alpha = .025$

Numerator Degrees of freedom

ν_2 \ ν_1	1	2	3	4	5	6	7	8	9	10	12	15	20	24	30	40	60
1	648	800	864	900	922	937	948	957	963	969	977	985	993	997	1001	1006	1010
2	38.5	39.0	39.2	39.3	39.3	39.3	39.4	39.4	39.4	39.4	39.4	39.4	39.5	39.5	39.5	39.5	39.5
3	17.4	16.0	15.4	15.1	14.9	14.7	14.6	14.5	14.5	14.4	14.3	14.3	14.2	14.1	14.1	14.0	14.0
4	12.2	10.7	9.98	9.60	9.36	9.2	9.07	8.98	8.90	8.84	8.75	8.66	8.56	8.51	8.46	8.41	8.36
5	10.0	8.43	7.76	7.39	7.15	6.98	6.85	6.76	6.68	6.62	6.52	6.43	6.33	6.28	6.23	6.18	6.12
6	8.81	7.26	6.60	6.23	5.99	5.82	5.70	5.60	5.52	5.46	5.37	5.27	5.17	5.12	5.07	5.01	4.96
7	8.07	6.54	5.89	5.52	5.29	5.12	4.99	4.90	4.82	4.76	4.67	4.57	4.47	4.42	4.36	4.31	4.25
8	7.57	6.06	5.42	5.05	4.82	4.65	4.53	4.43	4.36	4.30	4.20	4.10	4.00	3.95	3.89	3.84	3.78
9	7.21	5.71	5.08	4.72	4.48	4.32	4.20	4.10	4.03	3.96	3.87	3.77	3.67	3.61	3.56	3.51	3.45
10	6.94	5.46	4.83	4.47	4.24	4.07	3.95	3.85	3.78	3.72	3.62	3.52	3.42	3.37	3.31	3.26	3.20
11	6.72	5.26	4.63	4.28	4.04	3.88	3.76	3.66	3.59	3.53	3.43	3.33	3.23	3.17	3.12	3.06	3.00
12	6.55	5.10	4.47	4.12	3.89	3.73	3.61	3.51	3.44	3.37	3.28	3.18	3.07	3.02	2.96	2.91	2.85
13	6.41	4.97	4.35	4.00	3.77	3.60	3.48	3.39	3.31	3.25	3.15	3.05	2.95	2.89	2.84	2.78	2.72
14	6.30	4.86	4.24	3.89	3.66	3.50	3.38	3.29	3.21	3.15	3.05	2.95	2.84	2.79	2.73	2.67	2.61
15	6.20	4.77	4.15	3.80	3.58	3.41	3.29	3.20	3.12	3.06	2.96	2.86	2.76	2.70	2.64	2.59	2.52
16	6.12	4.69	4.08	3.73	3.50	3.34	3.22	3.12	3.05	2.99	2.89	2.79	2.68	2.63	2.57	2.51	2.45
17	6.04	4.62	4.01	3.66	3.44	3.28	3.16	3.06	2.98	2.92	2.82	2.72	2.62	2.56	2.50	2.44	2.38
18	5.98	4.56	3.95	3.61	3.38	3.22	3.10	3.01	2.93	2.87	2.77	2.67	2.56	2.50	2.44	2.38	2.32
19	5.92	4.51	3.90	3.56	3.33	3.17	3.05	2.96	2.88	2.82	2.72	2.62	2.51	2.45	2.39	2.33	2.27
20	5.87	4.46	3.86	3.51	3.29	3.13	3.01	2.91	2.84	2.77	2.68	2.57	2.46	2.41	2.35	2.29	2.22
21	5.83	4.42	3.82	3.48	3.25	3.09	2.97	2.87	2.80	2.73	2.64	2.53	2.42	2.37	2.31	2.25	2.18
22	5.79	4.38	3.78	3.44	3.22	3.05	2.93	2.84	2.76	2.70	2.60	2.50	2.39	2.33	2.27	2.21	2.14
23	5.75	4.35	3.75	3.41	3.18	3.02	2.90	2.81	2.73	2.67	2.57	2.47	2.36	2.30	2.24	2.18	2.11
24	5.72	4.32	3.72	3.38	3.15	2.99	2.87	2.78	2.70	2.64	2.54	2.44	2.33	2.27	2.21	2.15	2.08
25	5.69	4.29	3.69	3.35	3.13	2.97	2.85	2.75	2.68	2.61	2.51	2.41	2.30	2.24	2.18	2.12	2.05
26	5.66	4.27	3.67	3.33	3.10	2.94	2.82	2.73	2.65	2.59	2.49	2.39	2.28	2.22	2.16	2.09	2.03
27	5.63	4.24	3.65	3.31	3.08	2.92	2.80	2.71	2.63	2.57	2.47	2.36	2.25	2.19	2.13	2.07	2.00
28	5.61	4.22	3.63	3.29	3.06	2.90	2.78	2.69	2.61	2.55	2.45	2.34	2.23	2.17	2.11	2.05	1.98
29	5.59	4.20	3.61	3.27	3.04	2.88	2.76	2.67	2.59	2.53	2.43	2.32	2.21	2.15	2.09	2.03	1.96
30	5.57	4.18	3.59	3.25	3.03	2.87	2.75	2.65	2.57	2.51	2.41	2.31	2.20	2.14	2.07	2.01	1.94
40	5.42	4.05	3.46	3.13	2.90	2.74	2.62	2.53	2.45	2.39	2.29	2.18	2.07	2.01	1.94	1.88	1.80
60	5.29	3.93	3.34	3.01	2.79	2.63	2.51	2.41	2.33	2.27	2.17	2.06	1.94	1.88	1.82	1.74	1.67
120	5.15	3.80	3.23	2.89	2.67	2.52	2.39	2.30	2.22	2.16	2.05	1.94	1.82	1.76	1.69	1.61	1.53
∞	5.02	3.69	3.12	2.79	2.57	2.41	2.19	2.19	2.11	2.05	1.94	1.83	1.71	1.64	1.57	1.48	1.39

Bibliography

This understanding of how different parts of a business interelate and work together didn't just happen. It is the result of an accumulation of insights and learning gained from many sources. In looking back, four of these sources really stand out.

The richest is my own personal experience in the workplace. It has been enhanced by being able to manage a number of different responsibilities in four different industries. Having the opportunity to experience a large number of "at bats" was helpful and I was able to learn from the strikeouts as well as the hits.

The second source derives from what I have been able to learn from my supervisors, peers, and employees. There is no question that being able to observe their successes as well as their failures helped me envision an operating environment in which we could all be more effective.

The third was what I was able to learn from formal training in universities as well as targeted training programs. They were all instrumental in broadening my horizons.

The last source was the written word. Here I was able to get some different perspectives on a number of problem situations. They have helped shape my views on what separates a well run company from the rest and I believe have enhanced the practicality of this book. This bibliography is divided into the same planning, execution, control, and feedback sections as the book. This is a reference list for those who want to further explore these areas.

Planning

Ansoff, H.I., *Strategic Management*. London: Macmillan, 1979.

Bhide, A., *How Entrepreneurs Craft Strategies That Work*. Harvard Business Review, March-April, 1994.

Dertouzos, M.L., Lester, R.K., & Solow, R.M., *Made In America*. Cambridge, MA: MIT Press, 1989.

Drucker, P.F., *Concept of the Corporation*. New York: John Day, 1946.

_____, *The Age of Discontinuity*. London: Heinemann, 1969.

_____, *Management: Tasks, Responsibilities, Practices*. New York: Harper & Row, 1974

_____, *The Theory of Business*. Harvard Business Review, September-October, 1994.

Goddard, W.E., *Just-in-Time*. Essex Junction, VT: Oliver Wight Limited Publications, 1986.

Grenier, L.E., *Evolution and Revolution as Organizations Grow*. Harvard Business Review, July-August, 1972.

Kanter, R.M. *The Change Masters*. New York: Simon & Schuster, 1983

Kotter, J.P. *A Force for Change*. New York: Free Press, 1990.

Ling, R.C., & Goddard, W.E., *Orchestrating Success*. Essex Junction, VT, Oliver Wight Limited Publications, 1988.

Magee, J.M., *Decision Trees for Decision Making*. Harvard Business Review, July-August, 1964.

Orlicky, J., *Material Requirements Planning*. New York: McGraw Hill, 1975.

Peters, T., *Thriving on Chaos*. New York: Alfred A. Knopf, 1987.

Wight, O.W., *Manufacturing Resource Planning: MRP II*. New York: Van Nostrand Reinhold, 1981.

Executing the Plan

Argyris, C., *Organization and Innovation*. Toronto: Irwin, 1965.

de Bono, E., *The Use of Lateral Thinking*. London: Penguin, 1967.

Goldratt, E.M., *Cost Accounting is Enemy Number One of Productivity*. International Conference Proceedings, American Production and Inventory Control Society, 1983.

Goldratt, E., & Fox, R.E., *The Race*. Croton-on-Hudson, NY: North River Press, 1986.

Goldratt, E.M., & Cox, J, *The Goal*. Croton-on-Hudson, NY: North River Press, 1987.

Fazzi, R.A., *Management Plus*. New York: Irwin, 1994.

Hamel, G., & Prahalad, C.K., *Competing for the Future*. Harvard Business Review, July-August, 1994.

Larson, P.W., *MRP II Implementation in a Custom Printing Shop*. International Conference Proceedings, Society of Glass and Ceramic Decorators, 1991.

Naisbit, J., *Global Paradox*. New York: William Morrow and Company, 1994.

Schumaker, E.F., *Small is Beautiful*. London: Blond & Briggs, 1973.

Controling the Business

Adair, J., *Not Bosses But Leaders*. Guildford: Talbot Adair Press, 1988.

Bennis, W., *On Becoming a Leader*. London: Business Books, 1989.

Bonini, C.P., & Spurr, W.A., *Statistical Analysis for Business Decisions*. Homewood, IL: Irwin, 1973.

Bradshaw, P., *The Management of Self Esteem*. Englewood Cliffs, N.J.: Prentice-Hall, 1981.

Byham, W.C., *Zapp! The Lightening of Empowerment*. New York: Harmony Books, 1990.

Deming, W.E, *Improvement of Quality and Productivity Through Action by Management*. National Productivity Review, Winter 1981-82.

————, *Quality Productivity and Competitive Position*. Cambridge, MA: MIT, Center for Advanced Engineering Study, 1982.

————, *Out of the Crisis*. Cambridge, MA: Cambridge University Press, 1988.

Fellers, G., *The Deming Vision: SPC/TQM for Administrators*. Milwaukee: ASQC Quality Press, 1992.

Gordon, T., *Leader Effectiveness Training*. New York: Wyden, 1977.

Grant, E.L., Leavenworth, R.S., *Statistical Quality Control*. New York: McGraw Hill, 1980

Ishikawa, K., *What is Total Quality Control? The Japanese Way* Englewood Cliffs, N.J.: 1985.

Juran, J.M., *Quality Control Handbook*. New York: McGraw Hill, 1979.

Maslow, A.H., *Motivation and Personality*. New York: Harper & Row, 1970.

McGregor, D., *The Human Side of Enterprise*. New York: McGraw-Hill, 1960.

Skinner, B.F., *Beyond Freedom and Dignity*. New York: Alfred A Knopf, 1971.

Taylor, F. *Principles of Scientific Management*. New York: Harper & Row, 1947.

Wellins, R.S., Byham, W. C., & Wilson, J. M., *Empowered Teams.* San Francisco: Jossey-Bass, 1991.

Providing Feedback

Armstrong, D.M. *Managing by Storying Around.* New York: Doubleday, 1992

Greif, M., *The Visual Factory.* Cambridge, MA: Productivity Press, 1989.

Hale, R.L., Kowal, R.E., Carlton, D.D., & Sehnert, T. K., *Managing Supplier Quality.* Exeter, NH: Monochrome Press, 1994.

Harriman, B., *Up and Down the Communications Ladder.* Harvard Business Review, September-October, 1974.

Maurer, R., *Caught in the Middle.* Cambridge, MA: Productivity Press, 1992.

Meyer, C., *How the Right Measures Help Teams Excel.* Harvard Business Review, May-June, 1994.

Odiorne, G.S., *Discipline by Objectives.* Management of Personnel Quarterly, Summer, 1971.

Raia, A.P., *A Second Look at Management Goals and Controls.* California Management Review, Summer, 1966.

Schonberger, R.J., *Japanese Manufacturing Techniques.* New York: The Free Press, 1982.

Shingo, S., *The Sayings of Shigeo Shingo.* Cambridge, MA: Productivity Press, 1987.

Index

Push System 48, 57

Q

Quality Control 13

R

r Chart 163, 166, 214
Reasons for Failure 25
Red Line Indicators 267
Red Lined work areas. 266
Red Tags 269
Reducing Constraint
Influence 76
Risk, 38
Root Cause Analysis 196
Routings 21
Run 119
Runs Tests 119

S

s Chart 170
Sales and Operations
Planning 15, 17, 24
Sales forecast 16, 18, 20
Sales plan 15
Sales planning 17
Sample 92
Sampling 92

Seasonal operation 69
"Secret" customer 284
Secret knowledge 132
Self control 253
Shop floor control 49
Sigma 86, 95
Simulations 20, 24
Single Card Kanban 52
Single data base 19
Sorting operation 153
SPC 13
Special causes 108, 112, 192
Specification limit 92
Spider Chart 217
Staging areas 55
Standard containers 52
Standard deviation 86, 87, 99
State of statistical control 113
Statistical association 239
Statistical Process Control
13, 82
Statistical relationship 242
Statistical signal 143
Statistical variation 63, 83
Strategic vision 21
Systems 10

T

t 235
t test, 236